DK EYEWITNESS

TOP **10**
NORMANDY

T0054219

Top 10 Normandy Highlights

The Top 10 of Everything

CONTENTS

Normandy Area by Area

Streetsmart

Within each Top 10 list in this book, no hierarchy of quality or popularity is implied. All 10 are, in the editor's opinion, of roughly equal merit.

Title page, front cover and spine
Scenic view of Mont-St-Michel, Normandy
Back cover, clockwise from top left
Soft cheese, Honfleur; Natural cliffs, Étretat; Harbour, Honfleur; Mont-St-Michel; Rouen at sunset

The rapid rate at which the world is changing is constantly keeping the DK Eyewitness team on our toes. While we've worked hard to ensure that this edition of Normandy is accurate and up-to-date, we know that opening hours alter, standards shift, prices fluctuate, places close and new ones pop up in their stead. So, if you notice we've got something wrong or left something out, we want to hear about it. Please get in touch at **travelguides@dk.com**

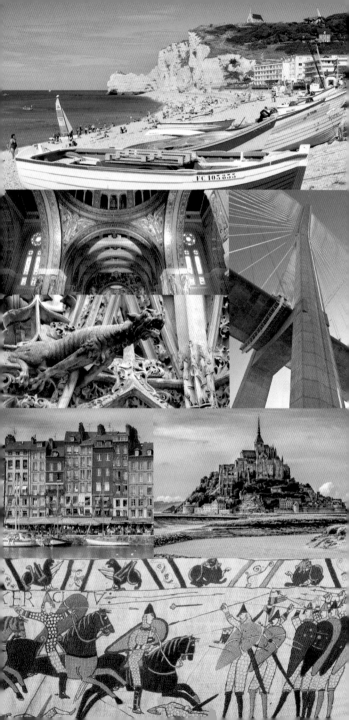

Welcome to
Normandy

Magnificent Gothic architecture, rugged coastlines, sublime châteaux, ancient sea ports, bucolic countryside, pungent cheeses and heady ciders. These are just a few of the attractions of Normandy, a region that has inspired countless artists and writers. With DK Eyewitness Top 10 Normandy, it is yours to explore.

Normandy's rich and fascinating history is most apparent in the stunning island monastery of **Mont-St-Michel**, the Gothic masterpiece of **Rouen cathedral** and the tale of the Norman conquest of England depicted in the exquisite **Bayeux Tapestry**. No less absorbing are the more recent traces of history seen in the **D-Day beaches**, with their poignant memorials and cemeteries. Normandy is also full of natural splendours. Its varied coast ranges from the spectacular cliff formations at **Étretat** to the vast beaches and remote headlands of the **Cotentin**. Inland, in the **Pays d'Auge**, you will find lush, rolling countryside full of orchards, cow-grazed meadows and handsome half-timbered manor houses.

A visit to Normandy also offers the chance to indulge in some fabulous seafood and fine cuisine, not to mention cheeses and cider. To work some of it off, you can cycle along idyllic tracks, walk through ancient forests, climb the wooded peaks of the **Suisse Normande** or ride a horse through the lovely **Perche** countryside.

Whether you're visiting for a weekend or a week, our Top 10 guide brings together the best of everything the region has to offer, from charming, rustic villages to elegant *belle époque* resorts. The guide has useful tips throughout, from seeking out what's free to finding places off the beaten track, plus six easy-to-follow itineraries designed to tie together a clutch of sights in a short space of time. Add inspiring photography and detailed maps, and you've got the essential pocket-sized travel companion. **Enjoy the book, and enjoy Normandy.**

Clockwise from top: **Boats on the beach at Étretat; Pont de Normandie; Abbaye de Mont-St-Michel; detail on the Bayeux Tapestry; Le Vieux Bassin, Honfleur; gargoyle at Notre-Dame, Louviers; interior of Basilique de Ste-Thérèse, Lisieux**

Exploring Normandy

Normandy features a scenic coastline, beautiful countryside and historic towns. To help make the most of your stay in this fascinating region, here are some ideas for two or seven days of sightseeing.

Dramatic cliff formations characterize the coastline at the resort of Étretat.

Two Days in Normandy

Day ❶
MORNING
Start in **Étretat** (see pp30–31), one of Normandy's most appealing seaside resorts, with its dramatic coastal formations, clifftop walks and enticing seafood restaurants.
AFTERNOON
Head to **Honfleur** (see pp20–21) and explore the picturesque harbour, lined with cafés and medieval houses. Don't miss the extraordinary wooden Église Ste-Catherine, the quirky Maisons Satie and Boudin's beautiful seascape pastels at the Musée Eugène Boudin.

Day ❷
MORNING
Immerse yourself in the **Pays d'Auge** (see pp38–9), with its meadows, orchards and half-timbered houses. Stop off at the pretty village of **Beuvron-en-Auge** (see p56), one of France's "plus beaux villages".
AFTERNOON
Head northeast to **Rouen** (see pp24–7) and admire its stunning Gothic

Cathédrale Notre-Dame and artfully restored medieval streets. There are some fine museums, notably the **Musée des Beaux-Arts** (see p55) and the **Historial Jeanne d'Arc** (see p26), which brilliantly tells the story of Joan of Arc.

Seven Days in Normandy

Day ❶
Follow Day 1 of the two-day itinerary.

Day ❷
Spend a relaxing morning in one of the seaside resorts on **La Côte Fleurie** (see pp32–3), perhaps Deauville or Trouville. After lunch, visit Cabourg, associated with Marcel Proust, and go fossil-hunting along the Falaises des Vaches Noires.

Day ❸
Tour the **D-Day Beaches** (see pp34–7). The broad Omaha Beach is particularly impressive; nearby are

Key
— Two-day itinerary
— Seven-day itinerary

Beuvron-en-Auge is one of the prettiest of the region's villages.

Étretat

SEINE-MARITIME

Trouville
Deauville
Falaises des
Vaches Noires
Cabourg
Honfleur

Abbey de
Jumièges
Rouen

Beuvron-en-Auge
Pays d'Auge

EURE

Giverny

Route du Cidre

CALVADOS

Roche d'Oëtre
Suisse
Normande

ORNE

Sées

Le Perche

Bellême

Stained-glass windows are a highlight at Bayeux's Cathédrale Notre-Dame.

two museums and the American cemetery. In the afternoon, drive inland to **Bayeux** *(see pp16–19)* to see its famous tapestry, as well as its lovely cathedral.

Day ❹

Start out early and head south to **Granville** *(see p105)*. Spend some time taking in the town's superb beaches and striking walled citadel. Afterwards, continue south to **Mont-St-Michel** *(see pp12–15)*, Normandy's most spectacular sight. Cross the footbridge and explore the abbey and the rest of the island.

Day ❺

Drive inland to **La Suisse Normande** *(see p95)*, a beguiling region of wooded hills and rocky crags. Climb up the Roche d'Oëtre for superb views of the Rouvre gorges. Pause for a spot of lunch, then continue east into the lush countryside of the **Pays d'Auge** *(see pp38–9)*, where Normandy's famous cheeses are made. Follow the Route du Cidre and end your day with a tour of a distillery.

Day ❻

Explore **Le Perche** *(see p112)*, an unspoiled region of undulating hills and woods, and stop off at one of its charming villages – perhaps **Sées** or **Bellême** *(see p114)*. Afterwards, immerse yourself in Claude Monet's exquisitely beautiful garden at **Giverny** *(see pp40–43)*.

Day ❼

Head northwest to the provincial capital of **Rouen** *(see pp24–7)* for a morning of sightseeing and shopping. Spend the afternoon wandering among the beautiful remains of the **Abbaye de Jumièges** *(see pp22–3)*.

Top 10 Normandy Highlights

The Porte d'Aval and the Aiguille d'Étretat

Normandy Highlights

Normandy brings a variety of images to mind: William the Conqueror, the D-Day landings, Mont-St-Michel, dramatic cliffs, summer beaches, sumptuous châteaux, historic abbeys, forested peaks, fruit orchards, Monet's garden. Whatever your list, it will barely scratch the surface of this rewarding region.

Mont-St-Michel ①

This solitary rock, dominated by a monumental abbey, became a place of pilgrimage over 1,000 years ago (see pp12–15).

② Bayeux Tapestry

This unique historical document and work of art tells the story of the Norman Conquest of England in 1066 (see pp16–17).

Port Racine
Cherbourg
Vauville
N13 Valognes
Les Pieux
Barneville-Plage
Carentan
Lessay
Marigny
St-Lô
Coutances
MANCHE
Granville
Mont-St-Michel ①
Avranches
Brécey
Le Teilleul

Baie de la Seine

D-Day Beaches ⑧
Arromanches-les-Bains
Ouistreha
Bayeux ②
Caen
Aunay-sur-Odon
CALVAD
Campeaux
Vire
Flers
Sourdeval
Domfront
La Ferté-Macé
Falais
Orne
ORNE

0 km 20
0 miles 20

④ Abbaye de Jumièges

These magnificent ruins – a blend of Romanesque and Gothic architecture – are all that remains of a 7th-century Benedictine abbey (see pp22–3).

Honfleur ③

A magnet for artists since the 19th century, this picturesque maritime town was also an important trade centre (see pp20–21).

5 Notre-Dame, Rouen

It took nearly 400 years to build this splendid Gothic cathedral, from the beautifully harmonious nave to the ornately carved west front *(see pp24–5)*.

6 Étretat

The cliffs of the Côte d'Albâtre are at their most stunning around this seaside resort, which has a collection of handsome medieval buildings *(see pp30–31)*.

7 Deauville and La Côte Fleurie

The resorts along this lovely stretch of coastline constitute a glamorous summer paradise *(see pp32–3)*.

8 D-Day Beaches

The Allied landings and the Battle of Normandy in 1944 are commemorated in museums, memorials and cemeteries throughout the area *(see pp34–7)*.

9 Pays d'Auge

Quintessential Normandy, this area is famous for its cider, cheese, gently rolling landscapes, orchards, and half-timbered manor houses *(see pp38–9)*.

10 Fondation Claude Monet, Giverny

The house where Monet lived for more than 40 years, and his stunning garden, are a tribute to the painter *(see pp40–43)*.

TOP 10 ⭐ Mont-St-Michel

One of the most spectacular sights in Normandy, this craggy rock crowned by a magnificent abbey appears to erupt from the surrounding landscape – a broad expanse of sand or sea, depending on the dramatic tides. The region's star attraction since pilgrims first flocked here 1,000 years ago, it now draws some three million visitors each year – and has perhaps 50 true inhabitants.

1 Abbey

This splendid building **(right)** is a pleasing jumble of architectural styles. Its jewel is the Merveille, built during the abbey's heyday and incorporating cloisters, the knights' hall, the refectory and the guests' room.

Ramparts 2

Punctuated by imposing towers **(right)**, the longest section was built to repel the English during the Hundred Years' War. The abbot's soldiers lodged in the Tour de l'Arcade.

3 Grande Rue

Through the fortified Porte du Roy, its portcullis still visible, the Grande Rue **(left)** winds steeply uphill. This pretty, narrow cobbled street was the original route used by pilgrims in the 12th century, and is still the way to the top of the mountain. These days, however, visitors have to run the gauntlet of souvenir shops and overpriced restaurants.

AN ISLAND

In 2014, Mont-St-Michel became an island again for the first time in more than a hundred years. As part of a major project aimed at restoring the "maritime character" of the Mont, the causeway that originally linked the island to the mainland was removed and a new wooden footbridge was built. The tidal waters can now flow freely, removing many years of built-up silt and sand. Visitors have to leave their cars on the mainland and cross the bridge either on foot, by bike or by shuttle bus or horse-drawn carriage. Note that the island itself is free to visit.

Map of Mont-St-Michel

5 km (3 miles)
15 km (9 miles)

5 Scriptorial d'Avranches
Films and games lead visitors through a celebration of the written word, from illuminated medieval manuscripts **(above)** to ebooks.

6 Archéoscope
A large model of the Mont rises from a huge tank of water in a spectacle of sound and light, with a historical commentary in English.

7 Église St-Pierre
The parish church, begun in the 11th century but not completed until the 17th, has an apse that straddles a narrow street. Its treasures include a silver statue of St Michael.

8 Chapelle St-Aubert
Legend tells of a huge rock blocking the entrance to a cave where the abbey now stands. Nobody could move it until a small boy miraculously pushed it into the sea with his foot. This tiny 15th-century chapel **(right)** occupies the site where the rock was supposed to have landed.

4 Ecomusée de la Baie du Mont Saint-Michel
This child-friendly exploration centre on the coast has models and interactive displays about the environment and wildlife of the bay, along with its history of fishing and salt production.

9 Logis Tiphaine
The chief of the king's armies Bertrand du Guesclin built this house in 1365 for his wife Tiphaine as a safe haven while he was away at war.

10 Musée Historique
Highlights are the garden periscope, a medieval monks' bath, 17th-century riding boots, and a re-creation of the abbey's prison cells.

NEED TO KNOW

MAP B5 ■ Office de Tourisme: Grande Rue ■ 02 33 60 14 30 ■ www.abbaye-mont-saint-michel.fr

Abbey: 02 33 89 80 00; open May–Aug: 9am–7pm; Sep–Apr: 9:30am–6pm (book ahead online); adm

Ecomusée de la Baie du Mont Saint-Michel: Rte du Grouin du Sud, Vains; 02 33 89 06

06; open Apr–Jun: 2–6pm; Jul–Sep: 10am–6pm; adm

Scriptorial d'Avranches: Pl d'Estouteville, Avranches; opening times vary, check website; adm; www.scriptorial.fr

Archéoscope: 02 33 89 01 85; open mid-Feb–Jun & Sep–mid-Nov: 9:30am–5:30pm; Jul & Aug: 9am–6:30pm; adm

Logis Tiphaine: 02 33 60 23 34; open 10am–5pm daily; adm

Musée Historique: 02 33 60 07 01; open Jan–Mar, Nov & Dec: 9:30am–5pm Fri–Tue; Apr–Oct: 9am–6:30pm daily; adm

■ Book a guided walk around Mont-St-Michel with Chemins de la Baie *(www.cheminsdelabaie.com)*.

Mont-St-Michel: Abbey Features

1 West Terrace
From this terrace, there are breathtaking views over the bay. On a clear day, you can see as far as the Channel Islands – the source of the granite used to build the abbey.

Key to Floorplan
▢ Church level
▢ Middle level

Chancel interior in the Abbey Church

2 Abbey Church
Despite its fine roof, the austere Romanesque nave – the oldest part of the church – is eclipsed by the fine Flamboyant Gothic chancel. The walls on the west front are scorched from a fire that broke out in the 19th century, when the abbey was used as a prison.

3 Cloisters
A garden enclosed by a double row of delicate pink granite columns, the cloisters gave the monks a place to meditate, converse and exercise.

4 Refectory
Apart from one monk, who would read aloud from the Scriptures, the monks ate in silence in this room, which has rows of narrow side windows invisible from the entrance.

5 Guests' Room
Light floods through large windows into this elegant rib-vaulted room, which was used for receiving important guests. Food was cooked in the two huge fireplaces.

6 Crypt of the Mighty Pillars
To support the new chancel, ten granite pillars were built in 1446 in this crypt, a room for those awaiting the judgment of the abbot, who presided over the courtroom next door.

7 St Martin's Crypt
Decorated with frescoes, this crypt, which provided the foundation for the south transept, was the funeral chapel for lay people.

8 Prison
During the French Revolution, the abbey began to be used as a prison. The iron cage used to confine dangerous prisoners is long gone, but the vast wheel for hoisting up provisions is still in place.

9 Knights' Hall
This vast, imposing hall was the monks' *scriptorium*, where they studied and copied manuscripts. A wooden trap door led to the food store.

The Gothic vaults of the Knight's Hall

10 St Etienne's Chapel
The monks' funeral chapel was well placed between the infirmary and the ossuary, where the bones of the dead were preserved. Monks kept vigil over the dead for three days and three nights.

ST MICHAEL AND ST AUBERT

According to legend, St Michael, the archangel, appeared three times in a dream to Aubert, Bishop of Avranches, commanding him to build an oratory on Mont Tombe (tomb on the hill). When Aubert delayed, the impatient archangel prodded a finger into Aubert's forehead, leaving a dent. Aubert built a small church in 708, which rapidly became a centre of pilgrimage for the *miquelots*, followers of the cult of St Michael, which had taken root in the West in the 5th century. The brightly gilded statue on top of the abbey spire, sculpted in 1897 by Emmanuel Frémiet, portrays the archangel in traditional, warlike fashion. Armour-clad, he is slaying a dragon (the symbol of the Devil) with his sword. In his other hand he carries a set of scales. This is a reference to the medieval belief that it was his role to weigh the souls on Judgment Day.

Frémiet's statue of St Michael on the abbey spire

TOP 10 EVENTS IN THE HISTORY OF MONT-ST-MICHEL

1 708: Aubert, Bishop of Avranches, builds an oratory on Mont Tombe

2 966: Duke Richard I imposes Benedictine rule

3 1017: Work on Romanesque abbey church begins; below, village slowly takes shape

4 1434: Ramparts completed during Hundred Years' War

5 1789: Monks leave; abbey converted to a political prison during the French Revolution

6 1874: Becomes a Historic Monument and opens to the public

7 1877: Construction of causeway connecting the Mont and the mainland

8 1969: Benedictine monks return and leave again in 2001

9 1979: UNESCO designates Mont-St-Michel a World Heritage Site

10 2014: Footbridge linking the Mont to the mainland completed, and opened to the public on 22 July

The archangel Michael is a warrior saint. Commanding the Army of God, he smites the Devil – in the form of a dragon – in the great conflict at the end of time. He is the patron saint of mariners in Normandy.

🔟⭐ Bayeux Tapestry

Both a unique historical document and an astonishing work of art, the Bayeux Tapestry tells the story of the Norman Conquest of England in 1066 – and it does so with thrilling narrative drive. Stitched in eight brilliant shades of red, yellow and blue wool, the 58 strip-cartoon-style scenes were embroidered just 11 years after the Conquest onto a single 70-m- (230-ft-) long linen cloth – at the behest, it is thought, of William the Conquerer's half-brother Odo, Bishop of Bayeux. It is displayed in a renovated seminary, along with helpful explanatory exhibitions and an excellent audio guide.

1 The Tapestry
The tapestry is displayed unfurled in a horseshoe-shaped gallery (above), with dim lighting to preserve its colours. The audio guide describes each scene, adding detail about the lifestyle of the period.

3 Harold's Mission to Normandy
In the first scene (left), Edward the Confessor is seen sending Harold from England to Normandy to tell Duke William that he will succeed to the English throne. Harold sets off for the coast.

4 William Invades England
As soon as William has ordered his invasion fleet to be built (No. 35) (above), the stylized trees that serve to break the tapestry's scenes cease to appear, and the story gathers pace.

2 The Tapestry Explained
Echoing the tapestry, an 85-m (280-ft) band of cloth explains the story. An English translation of the Latin text is shown beside images of each scene.

5 The Film
Maps and drawings depict the events of the Norman Conquest, and a film tells the story from the perspective of William's half-brother, Bishop Odo.

6 Harold's Oath

This critical scene (No. 27) provides the moral impetus for the story, told from the Norman point of view **(above)**: Harold, touching holy relics, swears his allegiance to Duke William.

7 The England of William

Using life-size figures, maps and scale models (including a delightful model of a village in Hampshire, England), William's influence on every sphere of English life after his conquest is cleverly portrayed.

8 Harold's Perjury

Harold returns to England from Normandy. On the death of Edward the Confessor, he is crowned king, breaking his oath to William. The appearance of Halley's Comet foretells his doom (No. 32).

9 The Battle of Hastings

The battle scenes **(below)** are marvellously depicted – full of the clash, clamour and bloody horror of medieval warfare (Nos. 51–58).

10 The Death of Harold

The tapestry comes to an abrupt end with the death of Harold and the victory of William over the English. The scene seems to support the legend that Harold was shot in the eye with an arrow.

NEED TO KNOW

MAP D3 ■ Office du Tourisme: Pont St-Jean; 02 31 51 28 28 ■ Centre Guillaume-le-Conquérant: Rue de Nesmond; 02 31 51 25 50 ■ www.bayeux museum.com

Open Times vary, check website; closed Jan

Adm: €9.50, concessions €5; under-10s free

■ For an excellent lunch, try Le Pommier *(Rue des Cuisiniers)* or Le P'tit Resto *(2 Rue du Bienvenu)*.

■ In July and August, the tourist office runs guided tours of the cathedral (€5) four times a day. The tours include the treasury room and the chapter house.

Museum Guide
The visit to the tapestry itself takes about 30 minutes: a slow-moving walkway takes you past the 58 tapestry scenes, with commentary in English for both adults and children from the audio guides provided. Afterwards, a film and exhibition provide interesting background information on the story of the Norman Conquest of England and the creation of the tapestry.

Sights in Bayeux

1 **Musée d'Art et d'Histoire Baron Gérard**

137 Rue du Bienvenu ■ Open May–Sep: 9:30am–6:30pm daily; Feb–Apr, Oct–Dec: 10am–12:30pm & 2–6pm daily ■ Adm ■ www.bayeux museum.com

The MAHB traces Bayeux's history through prehistoric finds, paintings, porcelain and lace. Highlights include a frescoed chapel.

Bayeux's Cathédrale Notre-Dame

2 **Cathédrale Notre-Dame**
Altered over time, the cathedral was consecrated in the presence of William the Conqueror in 1077.

3 **Musée Mémorial de la Bataille de Normandie**

Bayeux is the perfect base for visits to the D-Day beaches. This museum provides an excellent chronological introduction to the Battle of Normandy for all the family (see p36).

4 **Conservatoire de la Dentelle**

Maison Adam et Eve, 6 Rue du Bienvenu ■ Open 9:30am–12:30pm & 2–5:30pm Mon–Sat ■ www. dentellesbayeux.com

Visitors can enjoy watching a group of dedicated craftswomen at work as they continue the tradition of intricate Bayeux lacemaking.

5 **British Cemetery and Memorial**

The largest British war cemetery in Normandy contains 4,144 graves.

6 **The River Aure**
The banks of the River Aure supported many trades in the Middle Ages, including millers, tanners and dyers. A river path offers glimpses of this prosperous era, and passes through parks and play areas.

7 **Le P'tit Train**
From the cathedral and tourist office ■ 02 97 56 67 46 ■ Open Apr–Oct: several times daily ■ Adm

Discover the history and monuments of Vieux Bayeux during a 35-minute trip aboard the Little Train.

8 **Jardin Public de Bayeux**
55 Rte de Port-en-Bessin ■ Open Apr–Nov: 9am–8pm daily; Sep–Apr: 9am–5pm daily

A botanical garden with a weeping beech tree 13 m (40 ft) in diameter.

9 **Le Mémorial des Reporters**
Liberty Alley ■ 02 31 51 28 28

This memorial garden has 27 stone pillars inscribed with the names of over 2,000 journalists who have died covering conflicts since 1944.

10 **Vieux Bayeux**
Follow the way-marked route round the streets of old Bayeux, with information posts at points of interest.

Medieval Bayeux

WILLIAM THE CONQUEROR

A warrior through and through, William, Duke of Normandy and King of England, lived and died by the sword. Yet despite his appetite for battle (the Bayeux Tapestry illustrates some of his forays in Normandy), he had a statesmanlike ability to create order out of chaos. Having won the English crown, he made radical changes and improvements to society by fusing continental practices with native customs – in particular, instituting a type of feudalism that strengthened the monarchy, restrained the power of the Church, and supported the educational system of the day. With his wife Matilda, he founded some 30 abbeys, including the two at Caen (*see pp52–3*).

The Domesday Book, a huge and detailed record of English land ownership at the close of the 11th century, set the seal on Norman land reforms – and the occupation. It is now regarded as one of the most important documents in English history.

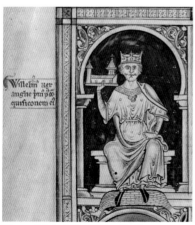

Manuscript depicting William the Conqueror

TOP 10
EVENTS IN WILLIAM'S LIFE

1 1027: Born in Falaise

2 1035: Receives the Duchy of Normandy on his father's death

3 1047: Helped by King Henri I of France, William crushes rebel barons in Normandy

4 1051: Edward the Confessor, his cousin, purportedly promises him the English throne

5 1064: Harold Godwinson – rival heir to the English throne – swears allegiance to William, perhaps through trickery or under duress

6 1066: Harold succeeds Edward as king of England

7 1066: William invades England, defeats Harold, and is crowned king at Westminster Abbey on Christmas Day

8 1072: Ruthlessly crushes all rebellions until England is conquered and united

9 1086: Commissions the Domesday Book, an invaluable survey of land ownership

10 1087: Dies in Rouen from a battle wound

TOP 10 ⭐ Honfleur

Seductively pretty, with cobbled streets and half-timbered or slate-fronted houses, Honfleur is a working port with a long maritime history. First mentioned in documents of the 11th century, by the 15th century it had become a significant fortified port. Its heyday came some 200 years later, when it spawned intrepid explorers like Samuel de Champlain, who set out from here to found Quebec. Le Vieux Bassin, the charming old dock at the heart of the town, is brimming with colourful sailing boats; artists have flocked here since the 19th century.

1 Le Vieux Bassin

This picturesque harbour **(below)** was built in the 17th century at the behest of Colbert, Louis XIV's chief finance minister, who also ordered the demolition of the ramparts. Quai Ste-Catherine is particularly attractive.

2 Musée Eugène Boudin

Now housing an exciting collection of 19th- and 20th-century art, the museum **(below)** was founded in 1868 by Honfleur's best-known artists, Boudin and Louis-Alexandre Dubourg.

3 Église Ste-Catherine

Built to replace a church destroyed in the Hundred Years' War, the largest wooden church **(right)** in France is half-timbered inside and out, with twin naves and tall oak pillars. The heavy bells required a separate stone bell tower.

4 Greniers à Sel

Larger cod catches in the late 16th century increased the demand for salt as a preservative. To accommodate this, two huge salt stores were built in the main street of the *enclos*, the walled town. Stone from the old ramparts was used for the walls, and oak for the roofs – which are still in superb condition. Now they are used for meetings, conferences, exhibitions and concerts.

Map of Honfleur

HONFLEUR ARTISTS

Turner, Corot, Courbet, Boudin, Daubigny, Dubourg, Jongkind, Monet and the Impressionists, the Fauves, Dufy, Friesz – these and countless others were drawn to Honfleur by the special quality of light in the Seine estuary, the unspoiled medieval town, and the beauty of the surrounding countryside – the same reasons that Honfleur has a thriving artists' colony today.

5 Église St-Léonard

From its 16th-century Flamboyant door to its 18th-century octagonal bell tower, St-Léonard is a hotchpotch of styles. The unusual copper lectern was produced in Villedieu-les-Poêles *(see p104)*.

6 Musée de la Marine

Housed in a 14th-century church, the Musée de la Marine **(above)** traces the history of the port through scale models, instruments, engravings, cutlasses, cannons and other fascinating artifacts.

7 Musée d'Ethnographie

Nine rooms crammed with objects, furniture and costumes transport you back through the centuries. The most delightful part is the haberdasher's shop, complete with ribbon samples.

8 Les Maisons Satie

A suitably offbeat tribute to the eccentric composer Erik Satie, born here in 1866. Videos, surreal room sets and life-size electronic sculptures re-create his fantasy world.

9 Chapelle Notre-Dame de Grâce

Explorers came to this enchanting little chapel **(right)** to pray before setting sail. Built in the early 17th century to replace a chapel that fell into the sea, it remains a place of pilgrimage.

10 Pont de Normandie

Opened in 1995, this elegant space-age bridge links Honfleur and Le Havre. Its 856-m (2,800-ft) span held the record – albeit briefly – for the world's longest cable-stayed bridge.

NEED TO KNOW

MAP F3 ■ Office du Tourisme: Quai Lepaulmier; www.ot-honfleur.fr

Musée Eugène Boudin: Pl Erik Satie; open Apr–Jun & Sep: 10am–noon & 2–6pm Wed–Mon; Jul–Aug: 10am–6pm Wed–Mon; Oct–Dec & Jan–Mar: 2:30–5:30pm Mon & Wed–Fri, 10am–noon & 2:30–5:30pm Sat & Sun; adm

Musée de la Marine/Musée d'Ethnographie: Rue de la Prison, off quai St-Etienne; open mid-Feb–Mar & Oct–mid-Nov: 2:30–5:30pm Tue–Fri, 10am–noon & 2:30–5:30pm Sat & Sun; Apr–Sep: 10am–noon & 2–6:30pm Tue–Sun; adm

Les Maisons Satie: 67 Blvd Charles V; open mid-Feb–Apr & Oct–Dec: 11am–6pm Wed–Mon; May–Sep: 10am–7pm Wed–Mon; closed Jan–mid-Feb; adm

■ In summer, enjoy a coffee at one of the pavement cafés in Le Vieux Bassin.

■ Audio guides can be hired for €5 from the tourist office.

TOP 10 ⭐ **Abbaye de Jumièges**

The hauntingly beautiful, bleached white ruins of this Benedictine abbey stand in a loop of the Seine. Founded by St Philibert in 654, following the donation of the estate to him by Queen Bathilde, wife of Clovis II, it was one of a number of abbeys built under the dukes of Normandy as the region turned to Christianity. Despite its chequered history (sacked by Vikings, it was rebuilt only to later be reduced to ruins and used as a quarry), it is a part of Normandy's rich heritage and an important stop on the famous Abbey Route.

1 Notre-Dame's West Façade

Stark and simple, Notre-Dame's impressive Romanesque west façade **(above)** was built around 1060, with a projecting porch flanked by two massive towers. Square at the base, octagonal above, they originally had wooden spires.

2 Storeroom

Once a welcoming hall for important guests, the storeroom, Gothic in design, Romanesque in decoration, is intact but for its ribbed vaulting.

The Abbey Grounds

3 Notre-Dame's Nave

Only the walls of Normandy's tallest Romanesque nave **(above)** still stand, left open to the skies after the demolition of the plaster vault that replaced the original wooden ceiling.

4 Notre-Dame's Transept

The west wall is all that survives of the 11th-century transept. The transept crossing was topped by a lantern tower, to let in the maximum amount of light in poor weather.

THE MAURISTS

After a period of spiritual decline in the 16th and 17th centuries, the Maurists, a fiercely intellectual and devout congregation of St Maur, founded in Paris in 1618, were dispatched to reform Jumièges Abbey. Among their improvements to its physical structure were a vast library, the abbey dwelling-house, and a monumental double staircase leading to a broad terrace and the gardens beyond.

5 Notre-Dame's Choir

Nothing remains of the earliest choir. The ruins **(above)** are from a 13th-century Gothic version, comprising an ambulatory with seven radiating chapels. An ornate rood screen is decorated with bas-reliefs illustrating the Passion of Christ.

6 Charles VII's Passage

This covered arcade, built in the early 1330s to link the two churches, predates Charles VII, but was named after a visit he made here with his mistress, Agnès Sorel, whose heart is buried under a marble slab in the north transept chapel.

7 Église St-Pierre

The western section of this church **(right)** was built in the first few decades of the 9th century, before the Viking raids on Jumièges. It is an important monument of the Carolingian period.

8 Chapterhouse

It was in this 11th- to 12th-century hall that a chapter from the rules of St Benedict was read out every morning, and monastic affairs were discussed. Between the 12th and mid-13th centuries, it became the abbots' burial ground.

9 Cloister

Today, the cloister **(left)** is an expanse of grass with a yew tree at its centre, but it was once the heart of the abbey, used by the monks for promenades, ceremonies, meditation and processions.

10 Abbey Dwelling-House

Northeast of the abbey ruins, this grand house **(below)** was built for François de Harlay de Champvallon, a "commendatory" abbot who was appointed directly by the king.

NEED TO KNOW

MAP G3 ■ 24 Rue Guillaume-le-Conquérant, 76480 Jumièges ■ 02 35 37 24 02 ■ www.abbayedejumieges.fr

Open Times vary, check website; closed 1 Jan, 1 May, 1 Nov, 11 Nov, 25 Dec

Adm: adults €7.50; students and pensioners €5.50; under-18s free

■ Stop for lunch at the Auberge des Ruines *(Place de la Mairie)*, opposite the abbey entrance.

■ You can hire tablets with a guide in English or download the free app. This includes 3D reconstructions of the abbey using augmented reality.

TOP 10 ⭐ Cathédrale Notre-Dame, Rouen

Located in the historic heart of the city, this magnificent cathedral took nearly 400 years to build. It stands as a record of the entire span of French Gothic architecture. Through the centuries, it has captured the imagination of artists, most famously Monet, who painted the west façade 30 times between 1892 and 1894 – at different times of day and year, and in various weather conditions, in order to capture the subtle changes of colour and light. His thick impasto suggests the texture of ornately carved stone.

1 West Façade

Familiar through Monet's paintings, this richly sculpted façade **(above)** reflects the evolution of the Gothic style. The most elaborate part is Roulland le Roux's early 16th-century central porch.

2 Booksellers' Courtyard

Created as a short cut for the local canons, this narrow courtyard is notable for the intricacy of its carvings.

3 Spire

Writer Gustave Flaubert was famously rude about it, but the people of Rouen have grown fond of this cast-iron spire **(above)**, the tallest in France. A bold 19th-century design, it matches the height of the hills surrounding the city.

Cathédrale Notre-Dame

4 Nave

Typical of the early Gothic style, this cathedral's exquisitely proportioned nave **(right)** has four storeys: arches, tribunes (in this case, false ones), a gallery and upper windows.

⑤ Lantern Tower

The tower rises a breathtaking 151 m (495 ft) above the transept crossing from floor to keystone, flooding the interior with light. At the base of each of its columns, busts 1 m (3 ft) high, said to represent the tower's builders, appear to be shouldering its weight.

⑥ Choir

The 13th-century choir is half-circled by tall pillars with vast carved capitals supporting pointed arches. The choir stalls, which are from the same period, are carved with comic scenes.

⑦ Lady Chapel

The delicate 14th-century Lady Chapel contains the tombs of more than 150 dignitaries, including the Tomb of the Cardinals of Amboise by le Roux.

⑧ Library Staircase

The lower two flights of this superb staircase (right) are the work of Guillaume Pontifs, while the upper two are 18th-century copies. The ogee arch above the wrought-iron door is typical Flamboyant Gothic.

⑨ Ambulatory Tombs

Here are effigies of Rollo, William Long Sword (known for his short stature rather than the length of his sword), and Richard the Lionheart, who ordered that his heart be buried in Rouen cathedral (see p47).

⑩ Window of St Julian the Hospitaller

In jewel-like blues and reds, this early 13th-century stained-glass window tells the tragic story of St Julian, who accidentally murdered his parents and founded a hospital in penance.

THE HISTORY OF THE CATHEDRAL

Building started in the mid-12th century on the site of two earlier cathedrals: the first, 4th-century; the second, an 11th-century Romanesque building from which the crypt survives. After a fire in 1200, work continued on the present building into the 16th century. Having survived the next four centuries more or less intact, it was devastated by bombing on 19 April 1944; only two flying buttresses prevented the whole building from collapsing. Repairs continue to the present day.

NEED TO KNOW

MAP M6 ■ Pl de la Cathédrale, 76000 Rouen ■ www.cathedrale-rouen.net

Open Apr–Oct: 9am–7pm Mon–Sat, 8am–6pm Sun; Nov–Mar: 2–6pm Mon & Sun, 9am–noon & 2–6pm Tue–Sat

For a tour of the city centre, the tourist office rents out audio guides for €5.

■ In a half-timbered building near the cathedral's north front, Dame Cakes (70 Rue St-Romain) has excellent tarts and gâteaux.

■ You can get a good view of the famous west façade from the tourist office (25 Pl de la Cathédrale).

■ Albane Courtyard reopened in 2012 after excavations, which uncovered relics of earlier cathedrals.

Other Sights in Rouen

Courtyard of Musée des Beaux-Arts

1 Musée des Beaux-Arts
MAP M5 ▪ Espl Marcel Duchamp ▪ Open 10am–6pm Wed–Mon ▪ www.mbarouen.fr

Highlights include paintings by Caravaggio, Velázquez, Monet, Géricault, Dufy and Modigliani.

2 Aître St-Maclou
MAP N6 ▪ 186 Rue Martainville ▪ Open 9am–7pm daily

This tranquil 14th-century courtyard was a plague cemetery. The timbered galleries are decorated with *memento mori* motifs.

3 Église St-Maclou
MAP N6 ▪ Pl Barthélémy ▪ Open Apr–Sep: 10am–noon, 2–6pm Sat–Mon (until 5:30pm Oct–Mar)

A masterpiece of the Flamboyant style of Gothic architecture.

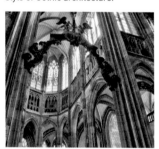

The vaults of Église St-Maclou

4 Le Gros Horloge
MAP L5 ▪ 191 Rue du Gros Horloge ▪ Open Apr–Sep: 10am–1pm & 2–7pm Tue–Sun; Oct–Mar: 2–6pm Tue–Sun ▪ Adm

The Great Clock has a panel showing the phases of the moon.

5 Église Ste-Jeanne d'Arc
MAP L5 ▪ Pl du Vieux Marché ▪ Open 10am–noon, 2–6pm Mon–Thu, Sat & Sun, 2–6pm Fri

The cross outside this modern church marks the site of Joan's martyrdom.

6 Musée National de l'Éducation
MAP N5 ▪ 185 Rue Eau-de-Robec ▪ Opening times vary, check website ▪ www.reseau-canope.fr/musee

This small museum charts 500 years of children's education.

Façade of the Palais de Justice

7 Palais de Justice
MAP M5 ▪ 36 Rue aux Juifs ▪ Closed to the public

The law courts are a splendid example of late medieval Gothic architecture.

8 Historial Jeanne d'Arc
MAP M5 ▪ 7 Rue St-Romain ▪ Open 10am–7pm Tue–Sun (last adm: 5:15pm) ▪ Adm ▪ www.historial-jeannedarc.fr

Multimedia displays trace the story of Joan of Arc in the archbishop's palace where she was sentenced.

9 Musée Le Secq des Tournelles
MAP M5 ▪ 2 Rue Jacques Villon ▪ Open 2–6pm Wed–Mon

The world's largest collection of historic wrought-ironware.

10 Musée de la Céramique
MAP M4 ▪ 1 Rue Faucon ▪ Open 2–6pm Wed–Mon

More than 6,000 pieces chart the history of Rouen's earthenware.

JOAN OF ARC

Although the facts of Joan's life are well recorded, she remains an enigma. The Maid of Orléans, as she came to be known, was from a pious peasant family, could barely read or write, yet succeeded in persuading the Dauphin to let her lead his army. The image of the androgynous, armour-clad Joan is iconic, portrayed through the centuries by sculptors, painters, playwrights and film-makers. While some critics have narrowed down her religious visions to psychiatric disorders, many others believe her to be a visionary. After her canonization, France adopted Joan as its patron saint, and her feast day (30 May) is celebrated throughout the country.

Joan of Arc's execution was meant to take place on 24 May 1431, but at the last moment she broke down and recanted. She later retracted that recantation, and met her fate on 30 May.

**TOP 10
EVENTS IN JOAN
OF ARC'S LIFE**

1 Born in Domrémy on 6 January 1412

2 Aged 13, hears voices for the first time

3 Four years later, the voices tell her to save France from the English

4 Gains an audience with Dauphin Charles on 9 March 1429

5 Leads the French to victory at Orléans (8 May); Charles' coronation follows (17 July)

6 Captured by the Burgundians in May 1430; they sell her to the English

7 Tried in Rouen for heresy and witchcraft, 21 February to 23 May 1431

8 Burned at the stake in Place du Vieux Marché on 30 May 1431

9 Rehabilitated in 1456

10 Canonized in 1920

Painting depicting Joan of Arc entering Orléans in May 1429

Following pages Abbaye de Mont-St-Michel

Étretat

Once a fishing village and then a popular seaside resort in the 19th century, Étretat is arguably Normandy's most alluring coastal town. Located on the Côte d'Albâtre (Alabaster Coast), it is flanked by two spectacular cliffs, the Falaise d'Aval and the Falaise d'Amont, each one hollowed out by the sea to form dramatic arches. Artists such as Courbet and Monet were beguiled by the play of light on these white cliffs and captured them many times on canvas.

1 Esplanade

Étretat has no port, just a restaurant-lined esplanade, curving along the seafront. It affords picture-postcard views of the dramatic cliff formations to either side, which have inspired countless painters over the years (pp48–9). If you come here for a stroll at dusk, you can see the cliffs spectacularly lit up.

2 Memorial to the Aviators Nungesser and Coli

Atop the Falaise d'Amont is a monument to French aviators Nungesser and Coli (above), who left Paris in 1927, hoping to make the first ever transatlantic flight. They never made it and were last seen over Étretat.

3 Porte d'Amont

Sculpted into the Falaise d'Amont, the cliff on Étretat's northeastern side, this natural archway was likened to an elephant dipping its trunk into the water by the author Guy de Maupassant. When the tide is out, you can walk along the beach almost to the foot of the arch.

4 Notre-Dame de la Garde

Perched on the edge of the Falaise d'Amont and with sweeping views out to sea, this mariners' chapel (right), originally dating from 1856, was destroyed in World War II and rebuilt in 1950.

5 Falaise d'Aval

On the south-western side of Étretat lies the Falaise d'Aval, with its natural waterfront arch (above). From the clifftop here, admire the "aiguille d'Étretat", a natural "needle" of rock rearing up out of the water.

Map of Étretat

6 Beach

Étretat's shingle beach (below) slopes steeply into the water. Wooden boats were once hauled up the beach to serve as bars in summer. Now some have been thatched over to become permanent restaurants.

7 Place Foch

The market square has some attractive half-timbered medieval buildings and a picturesque wooden market hall (above), which houses souvenir shops. Stalls are set up in the square every Thursday.

8 Belle Époque Villas

Étretat sports a number of grand houses, among them the Villa Orphée, built for composer Jacques Offenbach, and La Guillette, where Maupassant lived for a time.

9 Vélo-Rail Les Loges–Étretat

For a fun outing, cycle the 5-km (3-mile) railway track from Les Loges to Étretat in a pedal-powered vehicle, and return in an old diesel train.

10 Parc des Roches

Set atop the Falaise d'Amont, the Parc des Roches leisure park has a paddling pool for children, slides, a bouncy castle and miniature golf. Grown-ups can relax enjoying the panoramic views out to sea.

TOP10 ⭐ Deauville and La Côte Fleurie

Between Honfleur and Cabourg, the Norman coastline becomes a playground of resorts, casinos, watersport, sunshine and sandy beaches backed by wooded hills. It all started in Trouville, which triggered the 19th-century rage for sea bathing. Next came racy, romantic Deauville – created in the 1860s by a trio of wealthy entrepreneurs, and embellished in 1910 with a boardwalk, casino and racecourse. In contrast, Touques and Dives-sur-Mer have historic links with William the Conqueror, while stately Cabourg will be forever associated with Marcel Proust.

2 Touques

The vestiges of William the Conqueror's castle can be visited at Bonneville, above the port of Touques. In the neat town centre stands the 11th-century church of St-Pierre, with its unusual octagonal lantern.

3 Trouville-sur-Mer

In contrast to its neighbour Deauville, the town of Trouville (below) exudes a happy-go-lucky air. Attractions include its south-facing waterfront boulevard, trawlers and fish market, children's amusements and the wonderfully florid 1912 casino and town hall.

1 Deauville

Racehorses pounding the beach at sunrise, a glamorous wooden boardwalk, a glittering casino, the sumptuous Hôtel Normandy, the Bar du Soleil, the Pompeian Baths, designer shops, marinas, extravagant mock-Tudor villas (above): this is the epitome of an up-market seaside resort.

4 Villers-sur-Mer

This resort **(above)** is the starting point of the Vaches Noires cliffs, where many fossils have been found. The Paléospace l'Odyssée museum is devoted to these finds.

5 Villerville

In the summer months, this seaside town, surrounded by woods and meadows, organizes long nature walks along the coast.

6 Mont Canisy

Mont Canisy rises above Deauville, with views from Le Havre to the Orne; underground is a warren of German bunkers and tunnels.

7 Falaise des Vaches Noires

A walk at low tide between Villers and Houlgate takes you past the Vaches Noires cliffs.

THE HIGH LIFE

Deauville is well-known for its vibrant cultural scene which has been attracting holidaymakers since the 1800s. Throughout the year, the seaside resort hosts an array of events such as horse racing, film festivals, yachting regattas and vintage car rallies. The town's multidisciplinary arts centre, Les Franciscaines (www. lesfranciscaines.fr), brings the history of these events to life through a range of exhibitions dedicated to the town's cultural scene.

8 Houlgate

Like Villers-sur-Mer, Houlgate is a family resort notable for its Neo-Norman architecture – all half-timbering, gables, turrets and towers.

10 Dives-sur-Mer

The former port from which William set sail to conquer England features a magnificent oak-framed market hall **(left)** *(see p76)* and the church of Notre-Dame, founded in 1067.

9 Cabourg

Take tea at the Grand Hôtel **(right)**, vividly described by Proust in *A la recherche du temps perdu* and, like Cabourg itself, still redolent of those genteel 19th-century days.

NEED TO KNOW

MAP E3 ■ Office du Tourisme: Résidence de l'Horloge, Quai de l'Impératrice Eugénie, Deauville; www.indeauville. fr ■ Office du Tourisme: Jardins de l'Hôtel de Ville, Cabourg; 02 31 06 20 00

Paléospace l'Odyssée: Ave Jean Moulin, Villers-sur-Mer; opening times vary, check website; adm: €8.90, children €6.90; www.paleospace-villers.fr

■ In Deauville, Bar du Soleil on Les Planches and Bar de la Mer in the port are great for people-watching.

■ In Trouville, dine at one of the many water-front restaurants, such as Les Vapeurs *(see p99)*.

■ While access to Deauville beach is free, its pretty, colourful parasols, folded in a way unique to the town, are quite expensive to hire.

TOP 10 ⭐ D-Day Beaches

On 6 June 1944, Nazi-occupied France was invaded by British, American, Commonwealth and Canadian troops, resulting in the country's liberation. The Allied landings on the beaches of the Seine Bay (still known by their wartime codenames) and the ferocious Battle of Normandy that followed are commemorated today through a moving mixture of museums, memorials and cemeteries. Beautifully maintained and presented with great clarity, they give visitors a fascinating insight into the historic events of that momentous summer.

1 Utah Beach and Ste-Mère-Eglise
Over 13,000 US paratroopers were dropped into the Cotentin marshland (**above**); the US 4th Division came ashore and linked up with them.

2 La Pointe du Hoc
Preserved as it was at the end of fighting, this bleak headland was stormed by elite US Rangers using ropes and ladders to scale the cliff, with heavy casualties.

4 Batteries de Longues
Longues-sur-Mer
Near Arromanches, this is the only German battery still to have its guns. Its observation post (**above**), on the edge of the cliff, can also be visited.

5 American Cemetery
Colleville-sur-Mer
Formal and serene, the world's most visited war cemetery (**below**) contains 9,387 graves, a moving memorial and exhibits explaining Operation Overlord.

3 Omaha Beach
"Bloody Omaha" (**above**) saw terrible losses among the 1st and 29th US Divisions. A viewing table, two museums, 11 monuments and the American Cemetery tell the story.

6 Arromanches

The remains of the artificial Mulberry Harbour **(above)** make a startling sight – a testament to the ingenuity of Winston Churchill, who realized that if the troops wanted to land, they would have to bring their harbours with them.

TOURING THE BEACHES

Drivers can follow two themed and signposted routes leading to the main D-Day landings which are backed up by information "totems" at each place of interest (look for the dove symbol). Additional information can be found at local tourist offices, where you will also find details of recommended bus and taxi tour operators, and on the Normandy Tourism Board website (www.normandie-tourisme.fr) and www.cheminsdememoire.gouv.fr.

7 Gold Beach

Soon after landing here, the British 50th Division took Arromanches, and Mulberry Harbour was put in place. A memorial was erected on a hill overlooking the beach in 2021 commemorating the 22,442 British soldiers who died here.

8 Juno Beach

Several small seaside resorts line the beach assigned to the 3rd Canadian Division. The Canadian cemetery, at Beny-sur-Mer, is a beautiful spot containing 2,048 graves.

9 Sword Beach

Though the Allies established the beachhead with relative ease, the vital objective of Caen was thwarted, and its inhabitants had to wait another 34 days for their city to be liberated.

10 Pegasus Bridge
Bénouville/Ranville

The first Allies to land in France were the men of the British 6th Airborne Division, who seized this strategic bridge **(below)**, renamed after their insignia.

NEED TO KNOW

MAP C3, D3 ■ Office du Tourisme: Pont St-Jean, Bayeux; www.bayeux-bessin-tourisme.com
■ Observation bunker, La Pointe du Hoc: open Apr–Oct: 9:30am–5:30pm daily; Jan–Mar & Nov–late Dec: 10am–4:15pm daily

■ La Marine at Arromanches, La Marée at Grandcamp-Maisy and Le Bistrot d'à Côté at Port-en-Bessin *(see p99)* serve great seafood.

■ Plan your route in advance. Perhaps start at the Musée de la Bataille de Normandie and end at Arromanches 360 *(see p36)*.

■ Tours are run by Normandy Sightseeing Tours and D-Day Landing Tours *(see p125)*.

D-Day Museums

Musée Mémorial de la Bataille

1 **Musée Mémorial de la Bataille de Normandie**
MAP D3 ■ Blvd Fabian-Ware, Bayeux ■ 02 31 51 46 90 ■ Open Feb–Dec: daily ■ Adm ■ www.bayeuxmuseum.com

A good place to start, this museum gives a great overview of the battle.

2 **Overlord Museum**
MAP C3 ■ Colleville-sur-Mer ■ Open mid-Feb–Dec: daily ■ Adm ■ www.overlordmuseum.com

An excellent collection of tanks, memorabilia and artifacts from both sides of the conflict.

3 **Musée Airborne**
MAP B3 ■ Ste-Mère-Eglise ■ Open Feb–Nov: daily

Shaped like a parachute, the museum commemorates the American paratroopers who were dropped behind Utah Beach.

4 **D-Day Paratroopers Historical Center & Dead Man's Corner Museum**
MAP B3 ■ Saint Côme du Mont ■ 02 33 23 61 95 ■ Open Apr–Sep: 9:30am–7pm; Oct–Mar: 10am–6pm ■ Adm

A simulated flight in the Stoy Hora C47 plane and Eisenhower's flight jacket are highlights of this museum.

5 **Musée des Épaves**
MAP C3 ■ Rte de Bayeux, Port-en-Bessin ■ 02 31 21 17 06 ■ Open May: Sat & Sun; Jun–Sep: daily ■ Adm

Find a fascinating collection of objects recovered from wrecked warships.

6 **Musée du Débarquement**
MAP D3 ■ Arromanches ■ Open Feb–Dec: daily ■ Adm

Built on the original site of Mulberry Harbour (see p35), this museum pays homage to the famous artificial ports.

7 **Arromanches 360**
MAP D3 ■ Arromanches ■ Open Feb–Oct: daily; Nov & Dec: Tue–Sun ■ Adm ■ www.arromanches360.com

Witness the events of D-Day in an extraordinary 18-minute film.

8 **Juno Beach Centre**
MAP D3 ■ Courseulles-sur-Mer ■ Open Feb–Dec: daily ■ Adm

A museum devoted to the Canadian Army's contribution to D-Day.

9 **Musée Mémorial Pégasus**
MAP E3, D3 ■ Ranville ■ Open Feb–mid-Dec: daily ■ Adm

A range of exhibits commemorate the British glider assault.

10 **Musée du Débarquement d'Utah-Beach**
MAP B3 ■ Ste-Marie du Mont ■ 02 33 71 53 35 ■ Open Jun–Sep: 9:30am–7pm; Oct, Nov, Jan–May: 10am–6pm ■ Adm

Set on a beach, this museum recounts the events of the US 4th Division landing on 6 June 1944.

Musée du Débarquement d'Utah-Beach

OPERATION OVERLORD

The planning, manufacture of armaments, and training of men for the epic Allied invasion of Normandy in June 1944, codenamed Operation Overlord, began in earnest in the winter of 1943. D-Day was planned for 5 June, but was delayed for 24 hours due to bad weather. The unfavourable conditions, and an expected attack elsewhere (on Pas-de-Calais, nearer to Britain), caught the Germans by surprise when dawn brought the vast Allied fleet to the sandy beaches of the Seine Bay, flanked by airborne forces to the east and west. "It was as if every ship and every plane that had ever been built was there," said one British soldier. "The beach was alive with the shambles and the order of war … there were dead men and wounded men and men brewing tea."

Once beachheads were established on Utah, Omaha, Gold, Juno and Sword beaches, initial penetration into Normandy was uneven. Cherbourg fell on 26 June, Caen not until 9 July. Fighting conditions were grim among the hedgerows of Le Bocage (see p104), and it was not until 21 August, after the Germans were cornered in the Battle of the Falaise-Mortain Pocket, that the Battle of Normandy was finally won. Paris was liberated on 25 August.

TOP 10
D-DAY STATISTICS

1 4,000 ships in the fleet
2 5,800 bomber planes
3 4,900 fighter planes
4 153,000 Allied troops
5 20,000 vehicles
6 11,000 Allied forces casualties
7 2,500 dead
8 2,052,299 men came ashore following D-Day
9 3,098,259 tons of stores
10 640,000 Germans killed, wounded or taken prisoner in the Battle of Normandy

A plane flies over the Normandy Beaches

Americans from the 1st US Infantry land at Omaha Beach, the largest of the assault beaches, on D-Day, June 6 1944. In the first wave of attacks 2,400 died.

🔟 ⭐ Pays d'Auge

Apple and pear orchards, thatched farmhouses and half-timbered manor houses tucked into the hills, fat brown-and-white cows, producers selling cider and cheese – all these and more can be found in the Pays d'Auge. Stretching north to La Côte Fleurie, and bisected by the River Touques, the region perfectly encapsulates the charms of Normandy. Top attractions include villages, châteaux and abbeys – and of course, a Camembert museum and a Calvados distillery.

Lisieux ①

The region's principal town is connected with St Thérèse, who achieved posthumous renown for her book *Histoire d'une âme* (Story of a Soul), and was canonized in 1925. More than two million people visit the Basilique Ste Thérèse **(right)** annually, making it the second largest pilgrimage site in France.

② Beuvron-en-Auge

One of the loveliest and most popular villages in the area *(see p98)*. Charming houses, each one striped with old beams and dripping with geraniums **(above)**, cluster around the main square.

③ Manoir de Coupesarte

A short track off the D47 brings you to the most romantic of all the Auge manors. It is privately owned, but you can enter the adjoining farmyard to see the late 15th-century timbered house.

④ Vimoutiers

In the centre of Vimoutiers is a statue of Marie Harel, the woman credited with inventing Camembert in the sleepy village of the same name *(see p114)*. The Musée du Camembert tells the story.

⑤ St-Pierre-sur-Dives

This market town huddles round its huge, sheltering church, all that is left of the rich Benedictine abbey that once stood here *(see p97)*. The monks originally constructed the town's venerable market hall *(see 76)*.

Map of Pays d'Auge

Honfleur
Deauville
Cabourg
Pont-l'Évêque
Cormeilles ⑨
⑦ Clermont-en-Auge
Beuvron-en-Auge
Lisieux ①
② ⑩
⑧ ③
St-Pierre-sur-Dives
⑤ Livarot
Vendeuvre
⑥ Vimoutiers
Camembert ④
Argentan

6 Château de Vendeuvre

This elegant 18th-century château **(above)** contains a museum of miniature furniture *(see p55)* and some delightful water gardens.

7 Clermont-en-Auge

Seek out St-Michel-de-Clermont, a charming chapel with a panorama of the Pays d'Auge and marshland beyond.

8 Château de Crèvecoeur-en-Auge

A rare chance to look inside a medieval lord's fortified, moated Auge manor. The former agricultural buildings house a museum of oil prospecting, connected with the Schlumberger Foundation.

9 Distillerie Busnel, Cormeilles

At this distillery, you can learn about the process of making the apple brandy Calvados – and, of course, you can sample the results.

THE CIDER ROUTE

If you like cider, you can do no better than to follow the signposted Route du Cidre, linking the Pays d'Auge's principal cider-making villages – such as the delightful Cambremer, Bonnebosq and Beuvron-en-Auge – by way of pretty backroads. The route also passes about 20 local producers (recognizable by the sign "Cru de Cambremer"), who offer tours of their cellars and tastings. Pick up the leaflet "Tourist Routes" at any tourist office.

---

10 Château St-Germain-de-Livet

A visit to this enchanting château feels like entering a private world. Outside, there are turrets, towers, timbers and cleverly patterned brickwork **(below)**; inside, you can see oak furniture, Renaissance frescoes and creaking floorboards.

NEED TO KNOW

MAP E3–4, F3–4

■ Office du Tourisme: 11 Rue d'Alençon, Lisieux; 02 31 48 18 10

Château de Vendeuvre: **MAP E4**; open mid-May–Jun & Sep: 2–6pm daily; Jul & Aug 12:30–6pm daily; adm; www.vendeuvre.com

Château de Crèvecoeur-en-Auge: **MAP E4**; open Apr–Jun & Sep: 2–6pm daily; Jul & Aug: 11am–7pm daily; Oct: 2–6pm Sat & Sun; adm

Distillerie Busnel: **MAP F3**; Cormeilles; 02 32 57 80 08; open Mar–mid-Nov: 10am–12:30pm & 2:30–6:30pm daily; mid-Nov–Dec: Sat & Sun; adm; www.distillerie-busnel.fr

Château St-Germain-de-Livet: **MAP F4**; open Apr–Oct: 11am–1pm & 2–6pm Tue–Sun; adm

■ **Beuvron-en-Auge** makes a good lunch stop, with plenty of choice, including the gastronomic Pavé d'Auge *(see p74).*

■ The sights listed here make an excellent circular driving tour.

TOP 10 ⭐ Fondation Claude Monet, Giverny

In 1883, while travelling between Vernon and Gasny, Monet spotted Giverny from a train window. It was love at first sight, and later that year he moved here with Alice Hoschedé, whom he married in 1892. He created an exquisite garden here, which he considered his masterpiece, a painting of dazzling colours created with nature. After his death, the house and garden fell into disrepair, but were beautifully restored by the Académie des Beaux-Arts. Both are a living memorial to Monet and his work.

1 Water Garden
The asymmetrical and iconic water garden (below) is a place for calm contemplation of nature, among a riot of rhododendrons, willows, water lilies and more.

2 Water Lily Studio
His sight affected by cataracts, Monet built this large, light studio between 1914 and 1916, to work on his water lily series. It now houses the shop of the Fondation Claude Monet.

3 Clos Normand
Monet's French-style garden is a triumph of colour and judicious planting, with flowers in bloom all season.

4 Pink House
In this charming stucco house, Monet entertained Cézanne, Renoir, Matisse and other artists of the time.

5 Japanese Prints
Monet's precious woodblock prints are hung in several rooms around the house, according to a plan drawn up by the artist himself.

6 Japanese Bridge
This famous, wisteria-draped bridge (above) reflects Monet's abiding interest in Japanese prints, many of which are in the Pink House collection.

Map of the Fondation

7 Sitting-Room Studio

Monet used to retire to his simply furnished studio **(below)** after dinner to relax, smoke, and re-examine his day's work.

8 Dining Room

Imagine Monet, together with Alice Hoschedé, her children, and visiting artists and friends, seated around the large dining table in this perfectly restored room, painted in two shades of yellow, with faïence plates and Japanese prints on the walls, and vestiges of the dinner service in two dressers.

9 Monet's Bedroom

The room where Monet slept for 43 years, and eventually died, still has most of its original furniture, including a fine 18th-century inlaid desk. Endearingly, Monet kept works by the artists he most admired in his bedroom, among them Cézanne, Renoir, Manet, Pissarro and Rodin – a collection now scattered worldwide.

10 Kitchen

Little seems to have changed over the past century in this delightful room **(above)** – an extension built by Monet, with blue-and-white-tiled walls, a handsome cast-iron range, butler's sink, terracotta floor, and burnished copper pots and pans.

NEED TO KNOW

MAP K4 ▪ 84 Rue Claude Monet, 27620 Giverny ▪ 02 32 51 28 21 ▪ www.fondation-monet.com

Open Apr–1 Nov: 9:30am–5:30pm daily

Adm: €11.50; students and children aged 7–17 €7, visitors with specific requirements €6, under-7s free

Musée des Impressionnismes: 99 Rue Claude Monet, 27620 Giverny; 02 32 51 94 65; open Apr–mid-Nov: 10am–6pm daily; closed 1 week in Jul; adm: €8.50; ages 12–18 €6; ages 7–11 €4.50; under-7s free; free first Sun of month; audio guides €4; www.mdig.fr

▪ For refreshments, try Restaurant Baudy *(81 Rue Claude Monet)*, or the café at the Musée des Impressionnismes.

▪ While booking in advance is not obligatory, it is advisable.

Sight Guide

From the entrance on Rue Claude Monet into an outbuilding, stairs lead down to the water lily studio. Outside is the Clos Normand. In the southwestern corner, an underground passage leads to the water garden and Japanese bridge. On entering the Pink House, beside the entrance, you must turn left and follow the circuit round from the small blue reading room to the sitting-room studio, then upstairs to the bedrooms. The tour ends with the dining room and kitchen.

Musée des Impressionnismes, Giverny

The vine-clad entrance to the museum

1 The Museum
In the heart of the village of Giverny, the Musée d'Art Américain was replaced in 2009 by a museum entirely dedicated to the Impressionist movement exhibiting outstanding 19th- and 20th-century artworks. The Musée d'Orsay in Paris is its main partner.

2 The Collection
The museum features temporary exhibitions on the theme of Impressionism. There is a small permanent display showing Monet's influence on other artists.

3 Impressionist Painters
The artistic impact of the Impressionist movement on the second half of the 20th century is explored, with works by world-famous and lesser-known artists.

4 The Building
Terraced into the hillside, with vine-clad roofs, the building was designed by Philippe Robert to blend in with its surroundings. Inside, there are three large exhibition galleries and a 200-seat auditorium, used for conferences.

5 Exhibitions
The museum houses about two exhibitions each year, mostly showcasing works on loan from the Musée d'Orsay and from private collections.

6 Museum Gardens
In landscape architect Mark Rudkin's design, flowerbeds are planted simply in monochromatic colour schemes, divided by hedges. In 2006, the gardens were awarded Jardin Remarquable status.

7 La Brasserie des Artistes
Enjoy quiches, salads, grilled fish and meat at this elegant café. There is also a tea room, and a pretty terrace in the heart of the garden.

8 The Hills of Giverny
At the back of the museum, a large meadow opens out onto a hill filled with poppies, daisies and cornflowers. This is the very landscape that inspired Monet. A walk through this meadow is a good way to immerse yourself in the Impressionist mindset.

9 Guided Tours
Informative audio and guided tours of the current exhibitions are available in French, German and English for groups. Tours for individuals are available (in French) once a month.

A guided tour of an exhibition

10 Concerts and Events
www.mdig.fr
From April to October, concerts and other events are staged in the auditorium and garden. Check the website for more details.

MONET AND IMPRESSIONISM

Claude Monet

As a child, Monet was encouraged to paint *en plein air* (outdoors). He subsequently found the established techniques of studio-painting inadequate for his purposes. Fascinated by the illusory effects of sunlight and the weather on his subjects, he strived to "capture the moment" with quick, bold brushstrokes, and was concerned more with effect than with sharp, naturalistic detail – a novel technique that did not endear him to the Salon despite his early success. His painting *Impression, Sunrise*, exhibited in a show with other sympathetic artists, led a critic to coin the term "Impressionism", and he was heralded as the father of the style.

Monet's discovery of Giverny coincided with a new energy and confidence in his painting. The colours in his carefully planned garden provided him with an ever-changing palette, and in the years he spent in Giverny, he painted his best-known works. Until then his life had been dogged by financial hardship and tragedy; at Giverny, he was solvent and successful for the first time.

**TOP 10
EVENTS IN
MONET'S LIFE**

1 1840: Born on 14 November in Paris

2 1858: Introduced to painting *en plein air* by Eugène Boudin

3 1866: Enjoys first success at the Salon

4 1870: Introduced to art dealer Paul Durand-Ruel

5 1871: Starts collecting Japanese prints

6 1874: Holds the first "Impressionist" exhibition with Renoir, Sisley and other artists

7 1883: Discovers Giverny and moves into the Pink House

8 1892: Starts work on the garden and Rouen Cathedral series; marries Alice Hoschedé

9 1916: Starts his famous *Water Lily* series

10 1926: Dies on 6 December at Giverny

Water Lilies, **Claude Monet**

The Top 10 of Everything

Interior of Abbaye-aux-Hommes, Caen

🔟 **Moments in History**

Gallic leader Vercingetorix surrendering to Julius Caesar

1 58–51 BC: Roman Invasion

By 56 BC the Romans had swept through the region, conquering the Celtic Gallic settlers. They built roads, viaducts and fortified settlements, including Rotomagus (Rouen) and Augustodurum (Bayeux).

2 911: Treaty of St-Clair-sur-Epte

By the early 10th century, the Carolingian King Charles the Simple realized that the Vikings, who had invaded in 800, would not go quietly, so he ceded Rouen and the east of the region to them, making their leader Rollo the first duke of Normandy.

3 1066: Norman Conquest

When Edward the Confessor died with no heir, his cousin William saw his chance to claim the English throne. He set sail on 27 September 1066, triumphed at Hastings on 14 October, and was crowned King of England on Christmas Day.

4 1204: Union of Normandy and France

Since the accession of Henry II, King of England and Duke of Normandy, the French had tried to wrest control of the duchy from England. They succeeded in 1204, when King John lost Normandy to Philippe Auguste.

5 1315: Normandy Charter

Signed by Louis X, this charter gave the region provincial autonomy, a sovereign court of justice in Rouen, and control over taxes. In return, local taxes were increased dramatically – amounting to a quarter of the country's tax bill.

6 1450: French Recovery of Normandy

In the final phase of the Hundred Years' War, the decisive Battle of Formigny saw the French use guns and heavy cavalry to inflict a major defeat on English archers.

The bloody Battle of Formigny

The battle marked the end of fighting in Normandy and led to its recovery by France.

7 1789: Caen Revolt

During the French Revolution, there were royalist pockets throughout Normandy, but Caen became a centre for the republican Girondin movement (many of whose members originally came from the Gironde). Like the republicans who stormed the Bastille, their Norman counterparts demolished the château prison in Rouen.

8 1940: German Occupation

On 7 June 1940, the German army marched into Forges-les-Eaux and, two days later, into Rouen. This was the prelude to four years of occupation, during which many local people were imprisoned, tortured, deported and executed.

German tanks in occupied Rouen

9 1944: D-Day

In June 1944, Norman beaches became the target for Operation Overlord (see p37). By 20 August, Allied forces were advancing towards Paris over the Perche hills. Rouen was liberated on 30 August.

10 2019: 75th Anniversary of D-Day

On June 6 2019, veterans and world leaders gathered in Normandy to mark the 75th anniversary of the D-Day landings.

TOP 10 HISTORIC CHARACTERS

Charles de Gaulle

1 Clovis
Merovingian King Clovis (465–511) founded the French state by defeating the Romans and uniting the tribes.

2 Rollo
After signing the Treaty of St-Clair-sur-Epte, Viking leader Hrølf (c 854–928) was named Rollo, and became the first duke of Normandy.

3 William Long Sword
Rollo's acquisitive warrior son (c 893–943) extended the duchy's boundaries by taking Cotentin and southern Manche.

4 William the Conqueror
William (1027–87), the illegitimate son of Robert the Magnificent, united Normandy and conquered England.

5 Matilda
While abroad, William left Normandy in the capable hands of his wife Matilda (c 1031–83).

6 Richard the Lionheart
Richard (1157–99) became duke of Normandy in 1189. In 1196, he built Château Gaillard to protect Rouen.

7 Joan of Arc
A country girl, Joan (1412–31) was called by angelic voices to save France from English domination (see p27).

8 Samuel de Champlain
Explorer de Champlain (1567–1635) founded the city of Quebec.

9 Charlotte Corday
Educated in Caen, Girondin sympathizer Corday (1768–93) killed revolutionary Jean-Paul Marat in his bath.

10 Charles de Gaulle
Leader of the Free French, Charles de Gaulle (1890–1970) came ashore at Juno Beach on 14 June 1944 to reclaim France from the Germans.

🔟 Artists in Normandy

Mussel Collectors at Berneval,
Pierre-August Renoir

1 Pierre-Auguste Renoir
Monet's great friend and fellow Impressionist Renoir (1841–1919) did not discover Normandy until he came to the coast in 1879, the year he painted *Mussel Collectors at Berneval*. He became a regular visitor to Giverny.

2 Claude Monet
The founder and leading light of Impressionism was brought up in Le Havre. Having moved to Paris, he returned regularly to paint in Honfleur, Rouen, Étretat and Varengeville. In 1883 he settled in Giverny *(see pp40–43)*.

3 Jean-François Millet
Son of a peasant farmer in Gréville-Hague, Millet (1814–75) was apprenticed in Cherbourg before moving to Paris, where he worked under Paul Delaroche. He later moved to Barbizon, where he became a member of the Barbizon School led by Théodore Rousseau. He is best known for his gritty paintings of toiling farm workers.

4 Théodore Géricault
Born into a rich Rouen family, Géricault (1791–1824) shocked contemporaries with the realism and drama of paintings such as *The Raft of the Medusa*.

5 J M W Turner
The greatest English landscape artist of his time, Turner (1775–1851) paid frequent visits to Dieppe, Le Havre, Rouen and the Seine estuary. His vibrant watercolours had a profound influence on the young Monet.

Water Lilies, **Claude Monet**

6 Jean-Baptiste Corot

Corot (1796–1875) was a landscape artist who turned to portrait painting late in his career. The picturesque town of Étretat *(see pp30–31)* had particular appeal for him, and he travelled there with Courbet in the 1860s and 1870s.

7 Gustave Courbet

First of the French Realists, Courbet (1819–77) spent time in Trouville and accompanied Corot to Étretat. His stormy seascapes greatly influenced the Impressionists.

People on the Beach at Trouville, Boudin

8 Eugène Boudin

Brought up in Honfleur, Boudin (1824–98) did not have to go far to paint his seascapes. An advocate of painting in the open air – a practice he introduced to Monet – he was preoccupied with light and its effects on his subject matter. His loose brushstrokes heralded Impressionist techniques.

9 Georges Braque

Braque (1882–1963), who learned to paint while working for his decorator father in Le Havre, was attracted to the Fauve artists, but an encounter with Picasso transformed his style. In later years, he painted local landscapes and made stained glass in a studio in Varengeville.

10 Raoul Dufy

Only after flirtations with Impressionism and Fauvism did Dufy (1877–1953), a Le Havre native, find his own style. His subjects include carefree, ephemeral scenes, many in the coastal towns of Normandy.

TOP 10 PAINTINGS OF NORMANDY

The Gleaners, Millet

1 The Gleaners (Millet)
Painted in 1857. On show at the Musée d'Orsay, Paris.

2 Rouen Cathedral Series (Monet)
Painted between 1891 and 1895. One of the paintings is displayed in the Musée des Beaux-Arts, Rouen.

3 Impression: Sunrise (Monet)
Painted in Le Havre in 1872. Displayed in the Musée Marmottan, Paris.

4 Water Lily Series (Monet)
Painted between 1899 and 1926. A number of these paintings are on show at the Musée d'Orangerie, Paris.

5 The Cliff at Étretat after the Storm (Courbet)
Painted in 1869. Displayed in the Musée d'Orsay, Paris.

6 Wheat-field in Normandy (Dufy)
Painted in 1935. On show at the Musée Eugène Boudin, Honfleur.

7 People on the Beach at Trouville (Boudin)
Painted in 1865. Exhibited at the Musée Eugène Boudin, Honfleur.

8 View from the Port of Dieppe (Pissarro)
Painted in 1902. Displayed in the Château-Musée de Dieppe.

9 The Fish Market, Honfleur (Dubourg)
Painted in 1876. Displayed in the Musée Eugène Boudin, Honfleur.

10 View of the Coast of Normandy (Richard Parkes Bonington)
Painted in 1823. Exhibited at the Louvre, Paris.

🔟 **Writers in Normandy**

Gustave Flaubert

1 Gustave Flaubert

Flaubert spent the greater part of his 59 years in Normandy; its places and people suffuse his writing. Born in Rouen in 1821, he abandoned law training in Paris to live and write in Croisset until his death. He published his finest work, *Madame Bovary*, in 1857.

2 Guy de Maupassant

Maupassant (1850–93) was born at Château de Miromesnil near Dieppe, and spent his childhood in Étretat. His mother was a family friend of Flaubert, who would guide Maupassant's debut as a writer. His first masterpiece was *Boule de Suif*, published in 1880.

3 Marcel Proust

Proust was born in Paris in 1871 and died there in 1922. His *A la Recherche du Temps Perdu* is permeated by memories of Normandy – perhaps most notably the Grand Hôtel at Cabourg *(see p33)*, which he renamed Balbec.

4 Pierre Corneille

The classical dramatist Pierre Corneille (1606–84) was born in Rouen. His plays *Le Cid*, *Horace*, *Cinna* and *Polyeucte* formed the yardstick for French tragedy. *Le Menteur* is, however, a comic masterpiece. His writing often reflects the tension between regional and national loyalties.

5 André Gide

Born in 1869 to a Huguenot father and Norman mother, Gide spent the early and latter parts of his life in Normandy. He saw the realities of life here, first as mayor of a commune, and later as a juror in Rouen. He won the Nobel Prize for Literature four years before his death in 1951.

6 Alain Chartier

Poet and political writer Alain Chartier (c 1390–c 1430) was best known for *La Belle Dame sans Merci* – a poem on courtly love. Born into a distinguished Bayeux family, he wrote his earliest-known poem, *Livre des Quatre Dames*, after France's defeat at the Battle of Agincourt in 1415.

Jules Barbey d'Aurevilly

7 Jules Barbey d'Aurevilly

Barbey (1808–89), novelist, commentator, conversationalist – and as an admirer of Byron and Brummell, inveterate dandy – was still able to scandalize at 66, when he published *Les Diaboliques*. Born in St-Saveur-le-Vicomte, he was raised on a diet of Norman tales told by a family servant.

8 Robert Wace

What little is known about the poet Robert Wace (c 1115–c 1183) comes from his last work, *Roman de Rou*, a verse history of the dukes of

Normandy. Educated in Caen, he wrote his romances for the great and good living around this area.

9 François Malherbe

The classical poet Malherbe (1555–1628) left Caen to study in Paris, Basle and Heidelberg. He worked for Henri d'Angoulême (*grand prieur* of France and governor of Provence) for 10 years before returning home. Called to Court in 1605, he became the strict arbiter of French literary style.

François Malherbe

10 Jacques Prévert

Prévert (1900–77) visited Normandy in 1930 and fell in love with it. Soon after, he started to write poetry on the themes of beauty, innocence, love and despair. *Paroles*, his best-known collection, was published in 1945. In 1971, he and his wife bought a house in Omonville-la-Petite. They are buried nearby, and there is a memorial garden in St-Germain-des-Vaux.

Jacques Prévert

TOP 10 BOOKS SET IN NORMANDY

Annie Ernaux

1 A Woman's Story (Annie Ernaux)
A lovely tribute to the author's mother, who lived much of her life in Yvetot.

2 A Day in the Country and Other Stories (Guy de Maupassant)
Twenty-eight of Maupassant's brilliant short stories.

3 The Secret Life of the Seine (Mort Rosenblum)
The true story of a journey from Burgundy to Le Havre by houseboat.

4 Madame Bovary (Gustave Flaubert)
Set near the author's native Rouen, this classic ruffled contemporary feathers.

5 The Bayeux Tapestry (Wolfgang Grape)
The story of the Norman Conquest as told through the Bayeux Tapestry.

6 Mont-St-Michel and Chartres (Henry Brooks Adams)
A meditation on the medieval world, as seen through two of its most famous Gothic cathedrals.

7 D-Day: The Battle for Normandy (Antony Beevor)
A vivid and poignant account of the D-Day landings, packed with gripping biographical detail.

8 Gardens in Normandy (Valery, Motte and Sarramon)
A tour of forty spectacular gardens.

9 Chantemesle: A Normandy Childhood (Robin Fedden)
A lyrical account of an enchanted rural childhood in the region.

10 A Normandy Tapestry (Alan Biggins)
Biggins' account of his move to France with his family, which took him behind the scenes of French rural life.

TOP 10 Norman Abbeys

Le Bec-Hellouin monastery

1 Le Bec-Hellouin

In 1034, a knight called Herluin exchanged his charger for a donkey and founded a religious community on the banks of the River Risle. When he was joined some eight years later by the influential Italian theologians Lanfranc and Anselm, the monastery (see p78) grew to become the intellectual heart of Normandy. Disbanded during the Revolution and later demolished, it again became a Benedictine monastery in 1948.

2 Mont-St-Michel

Dramatically situated on a lone rock in the Bay of Mont-St-Michel, this famous medieval walled city (see pp12–15) is one of the most visited attractions in France.

3 Jumièges

A centre of learning for 700 years, monumental Jumièges (see pp22–3) became a quarry after the Revolution. Today, its enigmatic ruins, romantically set in a loop of the Seine, live again as one of the top "must-see" sights of Normandy.

4 Abbaye-aux-Dames, Caen

MAP D3 ■ Place Reine Mathilde

Like their founders William and Matilda, the Abbaye-aux-Hommes and Abbaye-aux-Dames (the first of the two to be built) are close cousins. The imposing convent buildings, built to accommodate girls from the Norman aristocracy, were designed by Guillaume de la Tremblaye.

5 St-Wandrille

Founded in 649 and rebuilt in the 10th century after destruction by Vikings, the abbey (see p88) became a centre of learning. Inevitably, the Revolution saw its demise, but in 1931 it became a Benedictine monastery again.

6 La Trinité, Fécamp

This vast, beautiful church (see p86) owes its scale to a casket containing the Holy Blood of Christ, said to have been washed ashore in the 1st century. The abbey, built on the spot between the 12th and 13th centuries, attracted streams of pilgrims. The relic, Le Précieux Sang, is still venerated today.

The striking Mont-St-Michel

7 St-Georges, St-Martin-de-Boscherville

In 1114, William of Tancarville founded a small community of monks, who took this beautiful Norman Romanesque building as their abbey church (see p88).

8 Abbaye-aux-Hommes, Caen

Lanfranc was the first abbot of the abbey (see p97), founded by William the Conqueror and consecrated in his presence in 1077. Ten years later, William was buried, most unceremoniously, in the abbey's church, St-Etienne.

Abbaye-aux-Hommes

9 Hambye

Lord of the Manor Guillaume Paynel founded the abbey (see p104) in 1145. Always a small community, its fortunes declined over the years, and in 1784 it was declared defunct. In the 19th century, the buildings were quarried for stone; only in the 20th century were the noble ruins visible today saved from further destruction.

10 La Trappe
MAP F5 ■ Soligny-la-Trappe

Founded in 1140, La Trappe was one of the Cistercian monasteries that adopted the Strict Observance – silence, prayer, abstinence, manual labour – introduced by the Abbot de Rancé in the 1660s. They were known thereafter as Trappist monasteries; there is another in the northwestern town of Briquebec.

TOP 10 RELIGIOUS FIGURES

Abbot de Rancé

1 Abbot de Rancé
Nobleman who renounced his former life and founded the Trappists in 1664.

2 St Philibert
Gascon court favourite and protégé of St Ouen, Philibert founded Jumièges in the 7th century.

3 St Wandrille
Nobleman founder of the abbey in 649. Known as God's True Athlete for his remarkable physique.

4 St Aubert
Bishop of Avranches, to whom, legend has it, the Archangel Gabriel appeared in 708, ordering him to build a chapel on Mont-St-Michel.

5 Lanfranc
Influential Italian lawyer-monk (1005–1089). Became William the Conqueror's archbishop at Canterbury.

6 St Anselm
Philosopher-monk (1033–1109) who joined Lanfranc at Bec and succeeded him as archbishop of Canterbury.

7 Joan of Arc
Teenage soldier (1412–31) who fought to save France from the English. She was captured and burned at the stake, but canonized in 1920.

8 Guillaume de la Tremblaye
Benedictine monk at Bec. A master architect and sculptor (1644–1715).

9 St Ouen
Credited with reviving Christian zeal in the Rouen region. As a result, several abbeys were founded.

10 St Thérèse Martin
Deeply spiritual young nun (1873–97), whose shrine at Lisieux is venerated.

🔟 Museums and Galleries

1 La Cité de la Mer, Cherbourg

MAP B2 ■ Gare Maritime Transatlantique, Cherbourg ■ Open Feb–Jun & Sep–Dec: 10am–6pm daily; Jul & Aug: 9:30am–7pm daily; book ahead online ■ Closed Jan & Mon in Mar ■ Adm ■ www.citedelamer.com

This former maritime station is home to Europe's deepest aquarium. A superb *Titanic* exhibition includes mock-ups of the interior of the ship. There's also a nuclear-powered submarine to explore. All of this introduces the visitor to the wonders of the underwater world, and to human adventures and achievements there.

Marine life at La Cité de la Mer

2 Le Mémorial de Caen

MAP D3 ■ Esplanade General Eisenhower ■ Open Feb & Mar: 9am–6pm daily; Apr–Sep: 9am–7pm daily; Oct: 9:30am–6pm daily; Nov & Dec: 9:30am–6pm Tue–Sun ■ Adm ■ www.memorial-caen.fr

A moving and contemplative museum of remembrance, the memorial takes the visitor on a journey through the causes and consequences of World War II and the ensuing Cold War, using a host of interactive and audiovisual techniques, as well as fascinating archive footage.

3 Musée des Impressionnismes, Giverny

This museum (see p42) is the only one in France that is wholly devoted to the influential Impressionist movement. It aims to explore the international nature of Impressionism.

4 Musée des Beaux-Arts et de la Dentelle, Alençon

MAP E6 ■ Cour Carrée de la Dentelle, Alençon ■ Open 10am–noon & 2–6pm Tue–Sun (Jul & Aug: daily) ■ Adm

In 1665, lacemakers in Alençon were given the challenge of creating lace equal in quality and popular appeal to that of Venice. They succeeded, coming up with a new and better technique, which made Alençon lace supreme until demand dropped in the 20th century. The story is told here, along with exquisite, intricate examples of the craft.

5 Musée des Beaux-Arts, Rouen

Monet's study of Rouen Cathedral and Corot's *Quayside Trade in Rouen* are among the highlights at this important art museum *(see p26)*. Its collection is strong on Old Masters, as well as the Impressionists.

6 Musée Eugène Boudin, Honfleur

Honfleur's rich artistic heritage is celebrated in this appealing museum *(see p20)*, which includes works by Boudin himself, as well as by Monet.

7 Musée Malraux, Le Havre

MAP E2 ▪ 2 Blvd Clemenceau, Le Havre ▪ Open 11am–6pm Tue–Fri, 11am–7pm Sat & Sun ▪ Adm ▪ www.muma-lehavre.fr

This innovative building, constructed from glass and metal, offers views of the port through a monumental concrete sculpture known as "The Eye". The museum spans five centuries of art history and is home to the second largest collection of Impressionist paintings in France.

8 Musée des Beaux-Arts, Caen

MAP D3 ▪ Le Château ▪ Open 9:30am–12:30pm & 1:30–6pm Tue–Fri, 11am–6pm Sat & Sun ▪ Closed Mon & public hols ▪ Adm ▪ www.mba.caen.fr

A superb collection of European paintings, dating from the 15th to the 20th centuries, is set in William the Conqueror's hilltop château. Perugino's *The Marriage of the Virgin* is a highlight.

9 Musée du Mobilier Miniature, Vendeuvre

This collection of 16th- to 19th-century miniature furniture *(see p39)* features meticulous craftsmanship.

Musée du Mobilier Miniature display

10 Bayeux Tapestry

Embroidered in 1077, this much-loved treasure *(see pp16–17)* recounts, with astonishing detail and drama, the story of Duke William's conquest of England. Galleries leading up to the tapestry bring the history vividly to life. The cloth itself – all 70 m (230 ft) of it – is behind glass.

Detail from the famous 70-m- (230-ft-) long Bayeux Tapestry

⓾ Unspoiled Villages

Granite houses lining the historic harbour at Barfleur

① Barfleur

The long tradition of fishing in Normandy is embodied in the charming port of Barfleur *(see p107)*. Brightly painted fishing boats jostle in the harbour, overlooked by stern granite houses braced for all weathers. Beaches and a lighthouse you can visit add to the appeal.

② St-Fraimbault
MAP D6

St-Fraimbault is a true *village fleuri*. Each spring, 100,000 flowers swamp the village in colour as villagers try to outdo each other's displays. It all culminates in a mid-August festival.

③ Lyons-la-Forêt

A captivating medley of 16th- to 18th-century half-timbered buildings, Lyons-la-Forêt *(see p87)* is set deep in the lovely Forêt de Lyons *(see p63)*. It starred in both the 1934 Jean Renoir and the 1991 Claude Chabrol film versions of *Madame Bovary*, whose intangible influence still permeates the area.

④ Beuvron-en-Auge

All the charms of the Pays d'Auge *(see pp38–9)* are to be found in Beuvron-en-Auge *(see p98)*. Its flowerdecked houses are prettily striped and patterned with timber. On the south side of the central square, the delightful 15th-century Vieux Manoir is elaborately decorated with wood carvings.

⑤ Putot-en-Auge
MAP E3

This sleepy Pays d'Auge village has little more than a church (with a fine Romanesque portal and a cemetery for Allied soldiers), manor house and little brick-built *mairie* (town hall), but it somehow encapsulates the rural delights of the Auge region. Nearby Criqueville-en-Auge is also worth a visit for its enchanting 16th-century manor house.

⑥ Montville
MAP G2

At the confluence of two rivers – Clérette and Cailly – Montville is distinctive for flowers and fire engines. A *village fleuri*, it has an attractive lake, a park with a superb 300-year-old purple beech, and the Musée des Sapeurs-Pompiers (Museum of the Fire Brigade). Full of

Picturesque Lyons-la-Forêt

old hand pumps and gleaming red fire engines, this fascinating museum traces the history of the French fire brigade from the early 18th century onwards.

Le Bec-Hellouin
MAP G3

A quintessential Norman village set among fields and apple orchards, Le Bec-Hellouin takes its name from the stream that runs beside it and from the Norman knight Herluin, founder of the impressive 11th-century Benedictine abbey. Half-timbered houses and colourful window boxes add to the charm.

8 St-Valéry-en-Caux
MAP G1

Encircled by high cliffs, this fishing village and child-friendly seaside resort occupies a charming spot on the Côte d'Albâtre (see p86), where tranquil Pays de Caux countryside meets beaches and boats. The village is also home to the Maison Henri IV, a fine timber-framed Renaissance house on the quay.

9 Allouville-Bellefosse
MAP G2

An extraordinary oak tree, thought to be at least 1,300 years old, has put this little village on the map.

Inside the huge trunk are a sanctuary and a hermit's cell fashioned by a local priest in 1696. Nearby, in an old farmhouse deep in the countryside, is the Musée de la Nature, with displays dedicated to the local landscape, flora and fauna.

Ancient oak at Allouville-Bellefosse

10 St-Céneri-le-Gérei
This enchanting village (see p114) has a memorable setting. Crowned by a fine Romanesque church, its stone houses overlook the gentle River Sarthe as it flows around a rocky promontory on the edge of the Alpes Mancelles.

Following pages Half-timbered houses at Le Bec-Hellouin

📖 Areas of Natural Beauty

River in La Suisse Normande

1 La Suisse Normande

Centred around the River Orne, this region *(see p95)* of gentle hills, rocky cliffs, woods and charming villages is hardly reminiscent of Switzerland, but still attracts its share of hikers and tourists. Well placed for exploring, the capital Clécy *(see p98)* is also a centre for climbing, canoeing and hang-gliding.

2 Pays d'Auge

When most people think of Normandy, they picture apple orchards, manor houses, rolling meadows dotted with cows, and timbered farmhouses. This is the Pays d'Auge *(see pp38–9)*, the rural hinterland to the Côte Fleurie, and home to cider, Calvados and some of France's best-known cheeses, including Camembert. It is also home to the Basilique Ste Thérèse de Lisieux, a long tradition of horse breeding, and *teurgoule* – a rice pudding.

3 Parc Naturel Régional de Normandie-Maine

Normandy's largest regional park *(see p112)* spans 2,350 sq km (900 sq miles) of Basse-Normandie and Pays de la Loire, with scenery that ranges from deep forests to gently rolling hills, and from marshland to meadows. The park aims to preserve rural traditions by promoting local arts and crafts, agriculture, forestry and outdoor activities.

4 Parc Naturel Régional des Boucles de la Seine Normande

MAP G2 ■ Maison du Parc: Notre-Dame-de-Bliquetuit ■ 02 35 37 23 16

Following the snaking loops *(boucles)* of the Seine, this 580-sq-km (224-sq-mile) park between Rouen and Le Havre was originally known as the Parc Naturel Régional de Brotonne. It embraces forests (notably the Brotonne), pastures and the Marais Vernier wetlands. It is also the starting point for the Route des Fruits, a picturesque 30-km (19-mile) cycle route through apple, pear, cherry and plum orchards.

5 Pays d'Ouche

MAP F5

As you journey from north to south, the landscape changes from the heavily wooded Eure to the lush green countryside of the Orne. Spanning both, the Pays d'Ouche is blessed with abundant streams, rivers and lakes, making it a paradise for anglers.

6 Pays de Caux

MAP G1–2, H1–2

Extending south from the striking white cliffs of the Côte d'Albâtre, and

Côte d'Albâtre, Pays de Caux

bordered by the fertile Seine and Bresle valleys, this immense chalky plateau provides wonderfully rich soil for arable farmland. You can catch glimpses of the farmsteads' half-timbered buildings and apple orchards through their massive stone gateways.

7 Parc Naturel Régional des Marais du Cotentin et du Bessin

MAP B3 ■ Maison du Parc: Les Ponts d'Ouve, St Côme du Mont ■ 02 33 71 65 30

The wetlands that characterize this park stretch 1,250 sq km (480 sq miles) from Les Veys to Lessay. The eastern marshes are home to many species of migrating birds and small mammals, which can be observed and studied from the park's hides and nature reserves.

8 Pays de Bocage

MAP C4

From the south of Cotentin down to southwest Calvados, this is an intensely rural and unspoiled stretch of countryside, much loved by ramblers – a patchwork of meadows, interrupted only by woods, rivers, picturesque villages and the distinctive network of hedgerows that gives the region its name.

Parc Naturel Régional du Perche

9 Parc Naturel Régional du Perche

MAP G6 ■ For information: Manoir de Courboyer, Nocé ■ www.parc-naturel-perche.fr

Between the Beauce plains and the Pays de Bocage, this 1,820-sq-km (700-sq-mile) park was created in 1998. The high ground is forested and the lower slopes are planted with orchards and hedges. Châteaux and manor houses pepper the landscape.

10 Pays de Bray

MAP H2

Formed by a geological fault known as the *boutonnière* (buttonhole), this is Normandy's least populated area. It contains the Béthune, Andelle and Epte rivers and rich dairy pastures.

TOP10 Forests

Reflections in the Étang de la Herse, Forêt de Bellême

1 Forêt de Bellême
MAP F6

This forest is dotted with large pools, including the lovely Étang de la Herse. Of its many splendid oak trees, the most famous is the Chêne de l'École on the western fringes – 40 m (130 ft) tall and more than 300 years old.

2 Forêt de Réno-Valdieu
MAP F6 & G6

Walk or cycle the path carved through the forest, and admire a magnificent line of giant oaks that soar up to 40 m (130 ft). They were planted in the 17th century, along with beech trees, to make planks for naval ships.

3 Forêt d'Eawy
MAP H2

Although the name Eawy (pronounced "Ee-a-vee") means wet pasture, this is a glorious beech forest covering 72 sq km (28 sq miles) on a jagged outcrop. It was originally planted with oaks, which were cut down to build houses after the Hundred Years' War. To see other species, follow the Chemin des Écoliers.

The breathtaking Forêt d'Écouves

4 Forêt d'Écouves
MAP E6

With its dense thickets of oak, beech, imported spruce and Scots pine, this is, at 140 sq km (54 sq miles), the region's largest and most beautiful forest. Its rich wildlife includes rare birds, deer and boar. The forest is also home to a 12th-century chapel, located in La Lande-de-Goult, which is known for its carved capitals.

⑤ Forêt de Brotonne
MAP G2

The heart of the Parc Naturel Régional des Boucles de la Seine Normande *(see p60)*, this forest of towering oak, beech and pine, almost encircled by a loop in the Seine and reached by the soaring Pont de Brotonne *(see p87)*, affords breathtaking views. It is home to deer, boar and hare, and in spring produces a carpet of bluebells.

⑥ Forêt d'Eu
MAP H1

This forest of beeches and many more exotic trees covers three large plateaus: Triage Forêt d'Eu, Haute Forêt d'Eu and Basse Forêt d'Eu. Among the highlights are a stunning view of the Yères Valley from Poteau de Ste-Cathérine, and a pair of intertwined oak and beech trees, known as the *bonne entente* (happy couple).

⑦ Forêt du Perche et de la Trappe
MAP F5

Glimpse the characteristic *étangs* (pools) through the trees from the D603, which bisects these two forests, usually regarded as one. A ramble here might turn into a mushroom hunt: the ferny floor is a breeding ground for ceps and chanterelles. Don't miss Abbaye de la Trappe *(see p53)*, home to Trappist monks.

⑧ Forêt de Roumare
MAP G3

With the Forêts de Rouvray, Verte and La Londe, Roumare forms a 140-sq-km (50-sq-mile) crown around Rouen. Roe and fallow deer and wild boar can be seen in the Parc Animalier (wildlife park). Near the park is Petit Charme Aboretum, which has walking trails running past 37 exotic species of tree.

⑨ Forêt de Lyons
MAP H3 & J3

This 100-sq-km (37-sq-mile) forest was a favourite hunting ground of Merovingian kings. Tall beech trees cast a beautiful, dappled light, making

Abbaye de Mortemer, Forêt de Lyons

it a great place for walking. In addition to Lyons-la-Forêt *(see p87)*, there are two châteaux and the ruined Abbaye de Mortemer to explore.

⑩ Forêt des Andaines
MAP D5

You might glimpse deer roaming through the forest that encircles Bagnoles-de-l'Orne, and you will certainly see different species of trees, including Japanese larch and Canadian fir. Try to visit the priory dedicated to St Ortaire, and the attractive observation tower of Bonvouloir.

Bonvouloir tower, Forêt des Andaines

Parks and Gardens

1 Château de Canon
MAP E4 ■ Mézidon-Canon
■ Open Apr & Oct: 2–6pm Sat & Sun;
May, Jun & Sep: 2–7pm Wed–Mon; Jul
& Aug: 10:30am–1pm & 2–7pm daily
■ Adm ■ www.chateaudecanon.com

The highlights of this elegant
18th-century Anglo-French park, are
the Chartreuses, a series of walled
gardens brimming over with flowers.
A pretty, Italianate château, statues,
a lake, a temple and a Chinese
pavilion add further interest.

Swans, Château de Canon

2 Le Jardin Intérieur à Ciel Ouvert
MAP D5 ■ Rue du Capitaine Martin,
Athis-Val de Rouvre ■ Opening times
vary, check website ■ Adm ■ www.
jardin-interieuracielouvert.com

The soothing sound of fountains and
running water forms the backdrop

of these enchanting gardens,
designed by sculptors Dominique
and Benoît Delomez.

3 Jardins de Bellevue
MAP H2 ■ Beaumont-le-
Hareng ■ 02 35 74 82 08 ■ Open
Mar–Nov: 10am–6pm Thu–Sun
■ Adm

Two national flower collections –
of *Meconopsis* (Himalayan blue
poppy) and *Helleborus Orientalis*
(Lenten rose) – are included in
these lovely year-round gardens
facing the Forêt d'Eawy (see p62).

4 Parc de Clères
MAP G2 ■ Clères ■ Open
Mar, Sep & Oct: 9:30am–12:30pm &
1:30–6:30pm Mon–Fri, 10am–6pm
Wed, Sat & Sun; Apr–Aug: 9:30am–
7pm Mon–Fri, 10am–7pm Wed, Sat &
Sun ■ Adm ■ www.parcdecleres.net

This landscaped park surrounds
the Renaissance château at Clères.
Created in 1920 by naturalist Jean
Delacour, the garden is populated
with flamingos and exotic ducks,
while in the park, animals such
as wallabies and gibbons roam.

5 Jardin Agapanthe
MAP H2 ■ Grigneuseville
■ Opening times vary, check
website ■ Adm ■ www.jardin-
agapanthe.fr

Winding paths lead through lush
foliage, over bridges, up and down

steps, and through a pergola. There is an elegant mix of exotic species, topiary and flowers.

6 Jardin des Plantes, Rouen

MAP G3 ▪ 114 Ave Martyrs de la Résistance ▪ Open 8:30am–dusk daily

These tranquil public gardens in the heart of the city house a large and important botanical collection, including formal flowerbeds, rare trees, hothouses, an orangery, a rose garden, a rockery, and a collection of medicinal plants.

Orchid, Jardin des Plantes, Rouen

Parc du Bois des Moutiers

7 Parc du Bois des Moutiers

MAP G1 ▪ Varengeville-sur-Mer ▪ Opening times vary, check website ▪ Adm ▪ www.boisdesmoutiers.com

British architects Edwin Lutyens and Gertrude Jekyll created the park and gardens for Guillaume Mallet, for whom Lutyens also built the house in 1898. Between here and the sea, the *valleuse* (dry valley) is filled with acid-loving plants such as rhododendrons and azaleas. Artists Cocteau, Monet and Braque were frequent visitors in their day.

8 Jardin d'Elle

MAP C4 ▪ Villiers-Fossard ▪ Open Mar–Nov: 9am–noon & 2–6pm Mon–Sat, 2–6pm Sun ▪ Adm ▪ www.delle-normandie.com

With a maze of individually themed areas, this modern landscaped garden has more than 2,500 varieties of plants and trees.

9 Le Jardin Plume

MAP H3 ▪ Auzouville sur Ry ▪ 02 35 23 00 01 ▪ Open mid-May–mid-Oct: 10am–noon & 2–6pm Wed & Sat, 2–6pm Thu, Fri & Sun ▪ Adm ▪ www.lejardinplume.com

This contemporary garden in a typical Normandy orchard contrasts formal, geometrically patterned *parterres* with swathes of tall grasses and flowerbeds overflowing with asters and Japanese anemones.

10 Château de Brécy

MAP D3 ▪ St-Gabriel-Brécy ▪ Open Easter–Oct: 2:30–6:30pm Tue, Thu & Sun (Sat in Jun) ▪ Adm

Five terraces of formal gardens sweep gracefully from the château towards the focal point: an ornate wrought-iron gate bearing the initials of Brécy's 17th-century owners. The gardens are thought to have been designed by François Mansart.

Aerial view of Château de Brécy

Spas and Resorts

Forges-les-Eaux
MAP H2

Quiet and dignified, Forges-les-Eaux became a fashionable spa town after it was visited in 1633 by a regal threesome: Louis XIII, his queen Anne of Austria, and Cardinal Richelieu. Today, the spa and casino, built in the 1950s, are run as a health and leisure complex.

Windswept, sandy Barneville-Plage

2 Barneville-Plage

Spectacular sandy beaches, backed by windblown dunes, sweep along the west coast of the Cotentin Peninsula, looking out towards the Channel Islands. At Barneville-Plage *(see p106)*, between Portbail and Barneville-Carteret, the coast becomes tame enough for a holiday beach, which is backed by lines of lovely villas.

3 Courseulles-sur-Mer
MAP D3

Along the Côte de Nacre at Juno Beach, where memories of the Normandy invasion *(see pp34–7)* mingle with modern-day seaside amusements, Courseulles has a large marina – although it is somewhat overshadowed by modern apartment blocks. The tourist office runs guided tours on the D-Day landings on foot, by bike and in sand yachts.

4 Bagnoles-de-l'Orne

Legend has it that medieval lord Hugues de Tessé left his horse Rapide to die quietly of old age in the forest, only for the animal to trot home in rude health. He found that a spring was the cause of the miraculous recovery, bathed there himself, and was also rejuvenated. Today, this calm, orderly spa town *(see p112)* attracts thousands to its Établissement Thermal, particularly helpful for rheumatism and circulatory problems.

5 Deauville and La Côte Fleurie

The magnificent coastline from Honfleur to Cabourg, with its series of wide, sandy beaches, means that all its resorts – Villerville, Trouville, Deauville, Villers-sur-Mer, Houlgate and Cabourg – have much to offer the sun-worshipper, with swimming and watersports all the way along. And if you tire of the beach, there are plenty of casinos where you can spend your money. Each place has its own character, none more so than exclusive Deauville *(see pp32–3)*.

Curving bay at Étretat

6 Étretat

With its shingle beach and esplanade curving between two famous chalk headlands (the Falaises d'Aval and d'Amont), its dramatic clifftop walks and its recreational Parc de Loisirs des Roches, charming and elegant Étretat *(see pp30–31)* is the Côte d'Albâtre's most alluring resort. Many writers and artists flocked here in the 19th century.

7 Granville

With its stern granite upper town on the one hand, and its beach and seaside amusements on the other, Granville *(see p105)* has two quite different faces. It became

fashionable as a resort in the 19th century. Among its current attractions, it features a thalassotherapy centre, the Aquarium du Roc (a "shell wonderland") and a lively casino.

8 Luc-sur-Mer
MAP D3

Thalassotherapy (seawater treatment) is a speciality of Norman resorts, and at bracing Luc-sur-Mer, the cure uses kelp extract. There's also a seawater hammam. Children can fish for crabs, shrimps and clams from the shore, and admire the skeleton of a 19 m (76 ft) beached whale in the attractive municipal park.

9 Riva-Bella
MAP E3

The people of Caen, on the River Orne, are proud of their close connection to the sea, and here, at the mouth of the river, is "Caen-sur-Mer": the attractive ferry and yachting port of Ouistreham and the bustling resort of Riva-Bella, with its superb sandy beach and jolly main street, Rue de la Mer.

10 Agon-Coutainville
MAP B4

With 8 km (5 miles) of fine, sandy beach, this west coast resort makes a great summer playground for the inhabitants of nearby Coutances and visitors alike. Spend a morning on the beach and then take an afternoon walk out to Pointe d'Agon, with its magnificent sea views.

Granville's upper town and harbour

⏏️🔟 Activities for Children

1 Parc Zoologique Cerza

MAP F4 ▪ Hermival-les-Vaux ▪ 02 31 62 17 22 ▪ Open Feb, Mar, Oct & Nov: 10am–5:30pm daily; Apr–Jun & Sep: 9:30am–6:30pm daily; Jul & Aug: 9:30am–7pm daily ▪ Adm ▪ www.cerza.com

To call Cerza a zoo is to do it a disservice. More than 50 hectares (123 acres) have been set aside to provide a natural environment for African and endangered species, including tigers and lemurs. It also oversees breeding programmes.

Giraffes, Parc Zoologique Cerza

2 Vélo Rail Experience

MAP D4–5 ▪ Between Caen and Condé-sur-Noireau ▪ 02 31 69 39 30 ▪ Open Apr–Oct (times vary, check website) ▪ Adm ▪ www.rails-collinesnormandes.fr

Ride a pedal-powered "bicycle train" and take in the spectacular scenery along the disused railway lines in the Orne and Noireau river valleys.

3 Parc de Loisirs L'Ange Michel

MAP C6 ▪ St-Martin-de-Landelles ▪ Open mid-Apr–mid-Jun & Sep: 11am–6pm Sat & Sun; mid-Jun–Aug: 10:30am–6:30pm daily; public hols ▪ Adm ▪ www.angemichel.com

Electric go-karts, "Aqua-splash" (boats that whizz down slides), dry-slope sledges and plenty more keep the children happy for hours here.

4 Étretat Aventure

MAP F2 ▪ Les Loges ▪ 02 35 29 84 45 ▪ Open Jul & Aug: 11am–7pm daily (times vary the rest of the year) ▪ Adm ▪ www.etretat-aventure.fr

In a lovely forest near Étretat, this treetop rope park has five exciting courses of varying difficulty – some suitable for children as young as 3 – high up among the trees.

5 Village Enchanté

MAP C5 ▪ Bellefontaine ▪ 07 61 13 40 64 ▪ Open Jul & Aug: 10:30am–6:30pm daily; May & Jun: 10:30am–6:30pm Sat & Sun ▪ Adm ▪ www.village-enchante.fr

A stunning park forms the setting for this fantasy village. Enchanted trails, bouncy castles and pony rides are aimed at the under-12s, with go-karts and zip wires for older kids.

6 Parc Zoologique de Champrépus

MAP B5 ▪ 493 Rue Saint-Gaud, Champrépus ▪ Opening times vary, check website ▪ Adm ▪ www.zoo-champrepus.com

This zoo aims to replicate the natural environments of around 60 different animals as closely as possible, including the endangered Sumatran tiger.

7 Musée du Chemin de Fer Miniature

MAP D4 ▪ Clécy ▪ Opening times vary, check website ▪ Adm ▪ www.chemin-fer-miniature-clecy.com

Visitors can admire one of Europe's largest model railways, and then take a miniature train ride around the site.

Musée du Chemin de Fer Miniature

Roller coaster ride at Festyland

8 Festyland

MAP D3 ▪ Caen-Carpiquet ▪ Open Apr–Jun & French school hols: 11am–6pm Wed, Sat, Sun & national hols; Jul & Aug: 10:30am–7pm daily; Sep: 10:30am–6pm Sat & Sun ▪ Adm ▪ www.festyland.com

With a roller coaster, water slides and a 3D cinema, this amusement park is for children of all ages.

9 Ludiver, Cap de la Hague

MAP A2 ▪ Flottemanville-Hague ▪ 02 33 78 13 80 ▪ Open Feb–Jun & Sep–Dec: 2–6pm Mon–Fri & Sun; Jul & Aug: 11am–6:30pm daily ▪ Adm ▪ www.ludiver.com

Enjoy experiences such as a 3D trek through the solar system and a journey to the centre of the Earth, or view images from the main (600 mm) telescope at Ludiver, which also has an observatory, a planetarium (book ahead) and a meteorology station.

10 Bâptemes Poneys, Haras National du Pin

MAP E5 ▪ Le Pin-au-Haras ▪ Opening times vary, check website ▪ Adm ▪ www.haras-national-du-pin.com

Where better to get up close to a pony than at the national stud farm. Children up to the age of 14 can go for a supervised pony ride, while more experienced riders can opt for a course with jumps.

TOP 10 TIPS FOR FAMILIES

1 Restaurants
Food outlets in Normandy are largely child-friendly, can provide high chairs, and offer an inexpensive *menu d'enfants*.

2 Picnics
A fun way to feed the family without having to worry about the mess. Pack picnic equipment and enjoy shopping for food at local markets.

3 Hotels
In most hotels, children under 12 can sleep in a bed in their parents' room at little or no extra cost.

4 Gîtes
For more space and flexibility, consider renting a house or apartment (see p127).

5 Car Travel
If you're renting a car, book child seats in advance. Stock up with water, food and games before journeys.

6 Trains
Under-4s travel free on French trains, as long as they sit on an adult's knee; 4- to 12-year-olds can usually travel for half the adult price.

7 Sightseeing
Children under 6 can visit many sights for free; tickets for under-12s are usually offered at a reduced price.

8 River Trips
Organized trips (see p125) with unique views of the countryside include those on the Douve and Taute in Cotentin.

9 Farms
See country life at close quarters at farms throughout Normandy. Check with tourist offices for more information.

10 Tourist Trains
A painless way to see the sights, these trains run through various town centres. Details are available from tourist offices.

Tourist train in Bayeux, Normandy

🔟 Outdoor Activities

1 Golf

Golfers are spoiled for choice in Normandy, which has 37 courses, 23 of them with 18 holes or more. Notable courses include Golf d'Étretat, situated on the clifftop above the famous Falaise d'Aval (see p30), and Golf de Saint-Saëns, with beautiful views over the Forêt d'Eawy (see p62). Deauville has no fewer than three top courses and there are fine courses at Omaha Beach and Granville.

Horse riding through the countryside

2 Bases de Loisirs

Normandy has many *bases de loisirs* (leisure parks) by lakes and on rivers, where you can enjoy swimming and watersports. Many also offer tennis, golf, riding, archery and other facilities.

3 Sand Yachting and Watersports

Normandy's broad, sandy beaches lend themselves perfectly to sand yachting (char à voile), particularly at Omaha Beach and along the west coast of the Cotentin Peninsula (there are large centres at Vauville and Portbail). You will also find windsurfing and kite-surfing on offer. Sailors can choose from around 100 sailing schools and clubs dotted along the coastline.

Catamarans for rent on a beach

4 Horse Riding

Normandy has many equestrian centres – especially in the Orne, where, for example, Le Village du Cheval (see p125) in St-Michel-des-Andaines offers a wide variety of horse-related activities. You can embark on a full-blown trekking holiday or just organize a few hours' riding through the countryside.

5 Canoeing

Condé-sur-Vire is Normandy's largest canoeing and kayaking resort; the Vire valley (see pp104–5) makes a perfect family outing. Canoeing is also on offer at Pont d'Ouilly in the Suisse Normande, on the Eure near Pacy-sur-Eure and at Saint-Saëns in the Pays de Bray.

6 Mountain Biking

The Perche is particularly suited to mountain biking, with marked trails at various levels of difficulty (maps are available from Mortagne-au-Perche and Domfront tourist offices). The terrain is also suitable in the Suisse Normande and at Amayé-sur-l'Orne.

7 Walking and Rambling

Normandy is wonderful walking country. Official footpaths (marked by red-and-white posts) crisscross the region, while the National Hiking Trails (Grandes Randonnées, or GR) provide spectacular long-distance routes. In Normandy, these include the

GR23 (Seine and Forêt de Brotonne), GR223 (Cotentin Peninsula coast) and GR221 (Suisse Normande).

8 Fishing

The diversity of Norman lakes and rivers makes freshwater fishing a popular pastime. Sea-fishing expeditions are organized from ports including Honfleur, Trouville, Dieppe and St-Valéry-en-Caux.

9 Bungee Jumping

MAP C4 ■ AJ Hackett Bungy: 02 31 66 31 66 (reservations required)

At the now defunct Souleuvre viaduct (built in 1889 by Gustave Eiffel), adrenaline junkies dive towards the ground secured by an elastic rope around the ankles, or scoot across the valley at 100 kph (60 mph) in a harness suspended from a cable.

Bungee jumping at Souleuvre

10 Cycling

Cycling is a great way to take in the Norman countryside. Each *département* has marked routes, with accompanying booklets available at tourist offices. In Manche, old railway lines and towpaths have been turned into cycle paths, while the forests of Lyons and Brotonne and the Eure and Seine valleys are excellent for cycling areas. The Veloscenic (www. veloscenic.com) route runs all the way from Paris to Mont-St-Michel.

TOP 10 WALKS

Hiking, La Hague Peninsula

1 La Hague Peninsula
The coastal path GR223 passes rugged countryside (see p103) and the dramatic Nez de Jobourg (see p107).

2 Val de Saire
This pastoral valley is a great place for a gentle country walk. Finish at St-Vaast-la-Hougue or at Barfleur (see pp106–7).

3 Dunes and marshes, Bréhal
MAP B4
Take the *route submersible* to see one of Cotentin's unique natural havens, Havre de la Vanlée – but be warned, the road becomes heavily flooded during the dramatic spring tides.

4 Waterfalls of Mortain
MAP C5
Follow the River Cance through the surrounding Alpine landscape.

5 La Suisse Normande
Rugged walking country, with great views from the Roche d'Oëtre (see p95).

6 Pays d'Auge
Rolling pastures, pretty villages, and plenty of stops for cheese and cider tastings (see pp38–9).

7 Forêt du Perche et de la Trappe
Combine walking with mushrooming amid woods and pools (see p63).

8 L'Aigle
Market day (Tue) is the best day for a walking tour of this historic town (see p114) and its neighbouring cantons.

9 Forêt d'Eawy
Explore one of Normandy's most beautiful beech forests by walking the Chemin des Écoliers (see p62).

10 The Seine
Follow the GR23 along the Seine's south bank and into the beautiful Forêt de Brotonne (see p63).

TOP 10 Culinary Highlights

Omelette de la Mère Poulard kitchen, Mont-St-Michel

1 Omelette de la Mère Poulard

Annette Poulard (1861–1931) was the *patronne* of a Mont-St-Michel hotel. The exact recipe for her famously perfect omelettes, available at any time to hungry visitors who crossed the bay on foot or by horse and cart, is not known. We do know that she never let the butter brown, beat her eggs vigorously in a copper bowl (possibly separating yolks and whites first), and stirred continuously as she cooked them in her long-handled pan.

Delicious *filets de sole Normande*

2 Filets de Sole Normande

Occupying pride of place among the catch brought back by Normandy's fishermen is the magnificent Dover sole, in French, *sole Normande*. It is equally delicious cooked simply *à la meunière* (with butter), or, as in Dieppe, with shrimps and mussels in a creamy *velouté* sauce – and can be prepared in countless other ways.

3 Poulet Vallée d'Auge

The key Norman ingredients, cider and cream, are combined to make this delicious chicken dish from the Pays d'Auge. Chicken pieces and mushrooms are sautéed in butter, then braised in a sauce of cider, Calvados and cream. Other traditional Norman dishes served in a sauce of cider and cream include *côtes de veau* (veal cutlets) and *filet de porc* (pork fillet).

4 Teurgoule

An enormously popular dessert, both at home and in restaurants, this regional speciality dates back to the days when spices, brought to Honfleur and Dieppe by merchant ships from the East, first became popular. Local housewives discovered that a flavouring of cinnamon was the perfect partner for pudding rice baked with cream, and the recipe for *teurgoule* was born.

5 Marmite Dieppoise

This hearty fish stew was originally concocted in Dieppe as a way of using up the many different types of fish, shrimps and mussels. It is lightly flavoured with spices.

6 Canard à la Rouennaise

Tasting much better than it sounds, *canard à la Rouennaise* refers to ducklings that have been dispatched by smothering; as a result, the blood is prevented from escaping, giving a strong flavour to the meat. Traditionally, the bird is stuffed, then served in a sauce made of its own liver and blood.

7 Tripes à la mode de Caen

A popular country dish in Normandy; tripe from the local cattle is cooked simply *à la mode de Caen* with onions, calf's feet, Calvados and cider, while in Ferté-Macé it is made into little bundles *en brochette* (on skewers).

8 Caille aux Monstrueux

There are many ways to cook this Elbeuf speciality made with quail and leeks. The variety of leek cultivated in the Seine and Eure valleys is known as *monstrueux* ("monstrous" – they are short and fat), and its distinctive flavour perfectly complements the quail.

9 Trou Normand

This famous Norman indulgence refers to a shot of chilled Calvados thrown back between courses to aid digestion. The word *trou* means "hole": the shot of *calva* is said to create a hole for more food.

10 Douillons and Bourdelots

Most often found in cake shops rather than in restaurants, these individual, melt-in-the-mouth pastries are filled with a whole small apple or pear, peeled and cored and flavoured with cinnamon.

A freshly baked apple *bourdelot*

TOP 10 CHEESES

A selection of Normandy cheeses

1 Camembert
This world-famous cheese was invented by Marie Harel during the Revolution. By the 1880s, equipped with its famous box and label, it was being exported all over Europe.

2 Livarot
Another cheese with a long history, it tastes a great deal better than it smells.

3 Neufchâtel
Dating back to the 10th century, this creamy cheese comes as a heart, or in one of five other shapes.

4 Pont l'Evêque
Originally called Angelot, this square, washed rind cheese, matured in wooden boxes, has a long history and dates back to the Middle Ages.

5 Pavé d'Auge
This square, spicy cheese from the northern Pays d'Auge was a forerunner of Pont l'Evêque.

6 Brillat-Savarin
A triple-cream cheese invented by cheese-maker Henri Androuët.

7 Fin-de-siècle
Despite its name, the history of this triple-cream cheese, promoted by Androuët, is unknown.

8 Fromage de Monsieur
A strong cheese invented near Rouen and sold by a man whose name really was M Fromage (Mr Cheese).

9 Coutances
Packaged in a round box, this rich, creamy cheese has a thin crust.

10 Briquebec
This mild cheese was invented in the 19th century by the Trappist monks of the Abbaye de Briquebec in the *département* of Manche.

🔟 Gourmet Restaurants

The elegant dining room at Manoir du Lys

1 Manoir du Lys, Bagnoles-de-l'Orne

A charming, old coaching inn, the Manoir du Lys is family-owned. It offers top-notch local cuisine with a contemporary touch (see p117). There is a good three-course fixed price menu with wines to match. The inn also organizes wine-tasting classes and "mushroom weekends".

2 La Marmite, Rouen

MAP L5 ■ 3 Rue de Florence ■ 02 35 71 75 55 ■ Closed Mon & Tue, Sun D ■ €€

An elegant little restaurant, off the tourist track, serving superb gourmet cuisine on a range of menus, including a seven-course *dégustation surprise*.

3 La Marine, Barneville-Carteret

Renowned chef Laurent Cesne has moved on, but his legacy of innovative and delicately prepared cuisine continues and promises a memorable gastronomic experience at this one-Michelin-starred restaurant. Enjoy a drink and take in the panoramic views out to sea while relaxing on the terrace (see p109).

4 Le Baligan, Cabourg

MAP E3 ■ 8 Ave Alfred Piat ■ 02 31 24 10 92 ■ Open daily ■ €€

This is an outstanding fish restaurant whose house specialities are fish soup and cod cassoulet. Attentive service, good ambience and tasty cuisine ensure that tables fill up quickly, so book ahead.

5 Ivan Vautier, Caen

This restaurant (see p99) is one of the best in Caen. Award-winning chef Ivan Vautier creates remarkable dishes paying homage to the best local produce. An extensive wine list is also available in a variety of vintages.

6 Le Pavé d'Auge, Beuvron-en-Auge

MAP E3 ■ Pl du Village ■ 02 31 79 26 71 ■ Closed Mon & Tue ■ €€

The former covered market of this picturesque village is the setting for Pays d'Auge's most sophisticated restaurant. The dishes here feature ingredients such as langoustines, asparagus and foie gras, which are served along with an excellent range of fine wines.

7 La Ferme Saint-Siméon, Honfleur

MAP F3 ■ Rue A-Marais ■ 02 31 81 78 00 ■ Closed Mon–Thu L ■ €€€

Experience the charm of this 17th-century Seine-side inn, once popular with Impressionist painters Monet and Courbet. Try the simple gourmet dishes prepared with high-quality and locally sourced ingredients.

⑧ Jean-Luc Tartarin, Le Havre

MAP E2 ▪ 73 Ave Foch ▪ Closed Sun–Tue ▪ www.jeanluc-tartarin. com ▪ €€€

Head chef Jean-Luc Tartarin has garnered high praise, as well as two Michelin stars, for his restaurant's innovative take on traditional French cuisine. Diners can choose either a three-course set dinner or go all out for the nine-course *dégustation*; try the seafood dishes, such as langoustine smoked with rosemary.

⑨ A Contre Sens, Caen

MAP M2 ▪ 8-10 Rue des Croisiers ▪ 02 31 97 44 48 ▪ Closed Sun, Mon & Tue L ▪ €€€

At the heart of Caen's old town, this wonderful restaurant draws on traditional Norman cuisine for its five- and seven-course surprise menus, which come with optional wine pairings. Vegetarian versions of the dishes are also available.

⑩ La Chaîne d'Or, Les Andelys

MAP H3 ▪ 25–7 Rue Grande ▪ 02 32 54 00 31 ▪ Opening times vary, call ahead ▪ €€

This charming 18th-century inn offers traditional cooking and fantastic river views. The excellent *menu dégustation* is very reasonably priced. Enjoy more than 350 varieties of wine here.

Classic decor at La Chaîne d'Or

TOP 10 NORMAN PRODUCE

Normandy apples and cider

1 Apples and Pears
Normandy's fertile soil supports countless varieties, which are used widely in cooking, and for cider, Calvados and sparkling *poiré*.

2 Vegetables
Manche is known for its superb carrots, leeks, radishes, shallots and parsley.

3 Dairy Products
The rich milk produced by Norman cattle makes velvety cream, butter (*beurre d'Isigny* is highly prized), and products ranging from Petit-Suisse cream cheese to *confiture de lait* – literally "milk jam".

4 Cheese
Four great soft cheeses – Camembert, Pont l'Evêque, Neufchâtel and Livarot – star on the Norman cheese board.

5 Agneau de pré-salé
Lamb raised on the salt marshes around Mont-St-Michel has a deliciously delicate flavour.

6 Boudin noir
Black pudding is the speciality of Mortagne-au-Perche *(see p81)*.

7 Andouille
Also famous is the black tripe sausage produced in Vire.

9 Fish
The Atlantic waters yield superb fish, supreme among which is the Dover sole (*sole Normande*).

9 Oysters
Norman oysters come from beds in one of three *crus*, or areas: Côte Ouest, St-Vaast-la-Hougue and Isigny.

10 Pork
Pale-fleshed Norman pork is a delicacy, particularly *porc de Bayeux*.

For a key to restaurant price ranges see p91

Markets

1 St-Lô
MAP C4

There's a typical market on Saturday mornings in the main square of this ancient town, where you can buy fresh produce from local farmers and fishermen from the stalls selling furniture, clothing and flowers.

2 Caen
MAP D3

Handsome 18th-century houses line Place St-Sauveur, the square in the centre of Caen where the pillory once stood, and where the colourful Friday market has been held since 1026. Stallholders sell traditional produce and, for early risers, an amazing selection of fresh fish.

3 Dives-sur-Mer
MAP E3

Stock up on regional produce at this traditional Saturday market in Dives, which takes place in the town's spectacular 15th-century timbered *halles* with its red-tiled roof.

4 Rouen
MAP G3

Place St-Marc is the scene of a lively market on Tuesday, Friday, Saturday and Sunday, with fresh produce, bric-a-brac and second-hand books. From late November, a Christmas market takes over Place de la Cathédrale.

Interior, St-Pierre-sur-Dives market

5 St-Pierre-sur-Dives
MAP E4

This inland town has a magnificent covered market hall. Dating from the 11th century, it was the largest medieval hall in Normandy. After it burned down in 1944, it was rebuilt in the style of the original, using hundreds of thousands of wooden pegs instead of screws and nails. Small local producers attend the busy Monday market.

6 Dieppe
MAP G1

Each Saturday, from 8am until noon, the long, pedestrian Grande Rue, lined with some 200 shops, becomes a massive open-air emporium.

Fruit and vegetable stall, Rouen market

Locals sell their produce (organic fruit and vegetables, *saucisses*, jams), professional retailers bring imports (olives, honey, cheeses) from every corner of France, and fishermen sell their daily catch. Dieppe is famous for its *lisettes* (baby mackerel), scallops and *gendarmes* or smoked herrings, which are available in November.

7 L'Aigle
MAP F5

This huge, bustling market dates back to the Middle Ages. Today, it draws thousands of people to L'Aigle every Tuesday. Hundreds of stalls, piled high with regional fruits and vegetables, cheeses and cider, are crammed into the town centre.

8 Forges-les-Eaux
MAP H2

An excellent farmers' market is held on Thursday mornings in the town centre and on Sunday mornings in Halle Baltard in this spa town on the Route du Fromage de Neufchâtel *(see p66)*. Stalls are crammed with organic dairy products, eggs, smoked meat and fish, jam and the Pays de Bray cheeses, including the famous Neufchâtel. On Thursday, there is a livestock market as well.

9 Cambremer
MAP E4

Local people dressed in peasant costumes, folk dancing, music-making and horse-drawn carriage rides are all part of the fun at Cambremer's market, staged every Sunday morning in July and August and on special occasions such as Easter, 1 May and Whit Sunday. Local producers mingle with regional craftsmen and artists.

10 Bayeux
MAP D3

One edge of the market that fills Place St-Patrice on Saturday mornings is given over to local smallholders selling their own fruit, vegetables, cheese, meats and also livestock (a few geese or chickens). The other stallholders are professional retailers, selling clothes as well as food.

Saucissons, Bayeux market

⓾ Normandy for Free

① Château d'O

Combining Flamboyant Gothic and Renaissance architectural styles, this splendid turreted château (see p113) is surrounded by a moat, a series of gardens, and stunning parkland. The house is occupied by the family that own it, but guided tours take in the courtyard and some of the grandest 18th-century rooms.

② Batterie de Longues-sur-Mer

The Batterie de Longues-sur-Mer (see p34) was a German defensive post during the war. Its observation post and guns are still intact, facing out across the Channel. Visitors are welcome to walk around and get a feel for the site.

③ Abbaye Notre-Dame, Le Bec-Hellouin

Visitors can wander for free around the tranquil grounds of the beautiful Abbaye Notre-Dame in Le Bec-Hellouin (see p97). The original medieval monastery – at one time the most influential abbey in Normandy – has largely been rebuilt since its destruction in the French Revolution, but the handsome 15th-century St Nicholas tower and various ruins still remain.

④ La Pointe du Hoc

A free visitor centre at La Pointe du Hoc (see p34) relates the dramatic landings made here by the Americans on D-Day. The site has been preserved unchanged since then and bomb craters still pit the ground.

Bomb craters on La Pointe du Hoc

The popular Le Tréport Funicular

⑤ Le Tréport Funicular

MAP H1 ■ Open mid-Jun–mid-Sep: 7:45am–12:45am daily; mid-Sep–mid-Jun: 7:45am–8:45pm daily (until 12:45pm Sat, 11pm Sun)

One of the most enjoyable things you can do in the pretty seaside town of Le Tréport (see p88) is take the funicular up to the top where you can enjoy the views of the town and the coast.

⑥ Les Jardins du Pontgirard

MAP F6 ■ Monceaux-au-Perche ■ Open mid-Jun–Sep: 10am–6pm daily

The restored gardens of the pretty Manoir du Pontgirard, surrounded by forest in the Perche countryside, are a delight, with their ponds, ancient trees and a wide variety of flowers, including lavender and dozens of types of euphorbia.

7 Cathédrale de Lumière, Rouen

Show daily: Jul 11pm; first half Aug 10:30pm, second half Aug 10pm; Sep 9:30pm ▪ www.rouentourisme.com

On summer nights, the façade of Rouen cathedral *(see pp24–5)* becomes the backdrop to a spectacular 30-minute video projection. Past themes have included the story of Joan of Arc, the Vikings and Monet.

8 Fromagerie Graindorge, Livarot

MAP E4 ▪ 42 Rue Général-Leclerc ▪ 02 31 48 20 00 ▪ Open Apr–Jun, Sep & Oct: 9:30am–1pm & 2–5:30pm Mon–Sat; Jul & Aug: 9:30am–5:30pm Mon–Sat, 10:30am–5:30pm Sun; Nov–Mar: 10am–12:30pm & 2:30–5:30pm Mon–Fri, 10am–1pm Sat ▪ www.graindorge.fr

At this long-established *fromagerie*, where Livarot and other Norman cheeses are made, you can watch the cheese-making process from windows looking out onto the factory (which operates only in the mornings). There is a tasting at the end of the tour.

9 Aître St-Maclou, Rouen

Built in the 16th century during an outbreak of the plague, the Aître St-Maclou *(see p26)* was a cemetery and charnel house. The courtyard looks very charming until you realize that the beams of the surrounding buildings are decorated with skulls and crossbones and chilling *danse macabre* imagery.

10 Théâtre Romain de Lillebonne

MAP F2 ▪ Pl Félix Faure 76170 Lillebonne ▪ 02 35 15 69 11 ▪ Open Mar–mid-Nov: 10am–noon & 1:30–5pm daily ▪ www.theatrelillebonne.fr

Lillebonne, on the banks of the Seine River, was a prosperous Roman port. Its amphitheatre, dating back to the 1st century, was unearthed between 1822 and 1840. The amphitheatre could hold up to 3,000 spectators. Further excavations in 2007 unearthed two more stages.

TOP 10 BUDGET TIPS

Market shopping in Honfleur

1 Weekly markets, held in many small towns and villages, are very good sources of affordable food, clothes, gifts and bric-a-brac.

2 Some museums are free on certain days; for example, the Musée des Impressionismes *(see p42)* is free on the first Sunday of the month. State museums are free for EU citizens under 25.

3 Set lunches at restaurants, especially at the high-end gastronomic establishments, can be very good value and cost less than the popular evening meals.

4 In Caen, Le Havre and Rouen, buy a carnet of bus/metro tickets rather than purchasing individual tickets.

5 In cafés, you can save money by avoiding the *terrasse*, which is more expensive than sitting at a table inside. Cheapest of all is standing at the bar.

6 Having breakfast at a café will usually cost less than at your hotel.

7 Many churches have free recitals and concerts. Tourist offices can provide details of these and other free events taking place in the local area.

8 Staying in a youth hostel, *chambre d'hôte*, a *ferme-auberge* (farmstay) or apartment can often be quite a bit cheaper than staying in a hotel.

9 In a restaurant you can cut costs by asking for *eau du robinet* (tap water) and wine or cider by the *pichet* (jug).

10 Admission to many museums and sights is free or reduced for under-18s, students and over-60s. In Caen, the free Caen pass from the tourist office gives reductions at a number of museums, restaurants and shops.

🔟 Festivals and Events

1 Cider Celebrations

A key part of Normandy's culture, cider is brewed across the region and, during the autumn apple harvest, many cider-filled events take place. The pretty town of Beuvron-en-Auge organizes the Fête du Cidre in October, which offers apple juice and cider tastings. Vimoutiers also hosts an apple festival in October which features a funfair as well as cider tastings and competitions.

2 Foodie Festivals

www.orbec.fr ▪ www.
pontleveque.fr ▪ www.mortagne-evenements.com

The region's beloved selection of home-grown cheeses are celebrated at an array of summer festivals. Lively fairs in Orbec, Pont-l'Évêque and Livarot are among the best – they offer a variety of cheese to try, including the famous Camembert variety. Meat-lovers will also enjoy Mortagne-au-Perche's spring fair, in March/April, which celebrates the local gourmet speciality – *boudin noir* (black pudding). Butchers gather to sell more than 5 km (3 miles) of this delicacy. Various competitions are organized including one to find the person who can eat the most *boudin*.

3 All that Jazz

www.jazzsouslespommiers.com

The annual Jazz sous les Pommiers (Jazz under the Apple Trees) has been running in Coutances for more than 30 years. Over one week in May, it features concerts by established artists, while also showcasing new talent. There are promenade concerts and street performances, as well as jam sessions.

4 Remembering D-Day

www.ddayfestival.com

To commemorate D-Day, Normandy hosts a programme of events in the weeks surrounding the anniversary (6 June 1944). Memorial gatherings take place, as well as fireworks, historical re-enactments and parades. Events are held all across the D-Day beaches and nearby towns.

5 Maritime Festivals

www.armada.org
▪ www.carnaval-de-granville.fr

In late June/early July every five or six years, the Rouen L'Armada hosts a fleet of tall ships and battleships from across the globe. The city buzzes with festivities, culminating in a colourful parade of boats down the Seine. There's also the Carnaval de Granville

***Boudin noir* displayed at Mortagne-au-Perche**

Sunset at Rouen's L'Armada

which began in the 16th century as a farewell party for local fishermen going out to sea. These days, people flock to see the decorated floats at this four-day Easter event. Another maritime event is the Fête des Marins in Honfleur, where local fishing boats meet in the Vieux Bassin on Whit Sunday to start their parade in honour of those who perished at sea.

6 Family Fun
www.rouen.fr ▪ www.dieppe-cerf-volant.org

Normandy is a great family holiday destination, with many festivals catered towards children. One such event is Rouen sur Mer: for three weeks in July the left bank of the Seine in Rouen is turned into a beach, with imported sand, deckchairs, beach umbrellas, giant waterslides and children's activities. On Friday evenings, there is also a live concert. In Dieppe, the September skies are filled with colour during the town's International Kite Festival. There are also kite-building workshops and flying classes on offer.

7 Horse Shows
www.polehippiquestlo.fr ▪ www.legrandcomplet.fr

A major event in the equestrian calendar, the Normandy Horse Show takes place in August, and includes auctions of horses, ponies and donkeys, as well as competitions. The showjumping and obstacle courses are the most popular. Spectators will have the opportunity to see a wide variety of different breeds, from sporting to cart horses. Haras

National du Pin *(p69)*, the oldest national stud in France, also puts on a show for the public in August.

8 On the Big Screen
www.festival-deauville.com

Although it is not quite as prestigious as Cannes, the Deauville American Film Festival is dedicated to the best American movies of the year and always attracts its share of Hollywood stars. The festival takes places in September, and awards are presented by an all-French jury. On a smaller scale, Rouen hosts the Ciné Friendly Film Festival in April to showcase a programme of LGBTQ+ films.

9 Agriculture Fairs
Normandy hosts a number of agriculture shows and fairs throughout the year. The biggest, and most well-known, is the Foire de Sainte-Croix in Lessay. Around 400,000 people gather on the second weekend of September for the fair; there are carnival rides and spit roasts, as well as exhibitors and livestock sales.

Spit roasts, Foire de Sainte-Croix

10 Christmas Festivities
Christmas markets pop up thoughout the region in December. The medieval town of Sées comes alive on the second Saturday in December for the Foire aux Dindes. People come from all over to see Normandy's largest turkey fair and preview their Christmas dinner. Honfleur, Le Havre and Rouen also host spectacular festive markets.

Normandy
Area by Area

Le Vieux Bassin, Honfleur

TOP 10 Northeastern Normandy

Gros Horloge, an astronomical clock in Rouen

Inland from the dramatic Côte d'Albâtre, with its harbours and seaside resorts sheltering between chalky cliffs, northeastern Normandy is dominated by the Seine, which follows a meandering course at its southern border. An unspoiled region of forests and rivers, it embraces the *département* of Seine-Maritime and – north of the Seine and reaching to the Epte – a slice of Eure. At the confluence of the two rivers is Giverny, the village made famous by Monet. Seine-Maritime has a varied landscape with the lush, sparsely populated Pays de Bray in the northeast and, at its heart, the limestone plateau of the Pays de Caux. Between the sea and the cultured cathedral city of Rouen, one magnificent abbey after another overlooks the wooded banks of the Seine Valley – spiritual stations on the well-trodden Abbey Route.

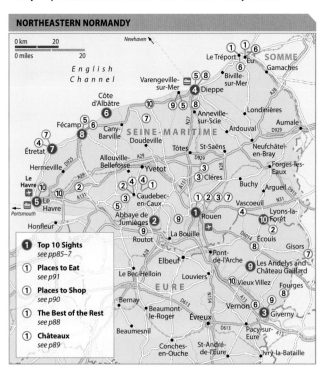

NORTHEASTERN NORMANDY

1 **Top 10 Sights**
see pp85–7

1 **Places to Eat**
see p91

1 **Places to Shop**
see p90

1 **The Best of the Rest**
see p88

1 **Châteaux**
see p89

The Seine winding through the historic city of Rouen

1 Rouen

Founded by the Romans in around 50 BC, the capital of Haute-Normandie occupied a strategic site on the Seine – the last point where the river could be bridged. From the end of the Hundred Years' War, Rouen prospered through textile production and maritime trade. The north bank's treasures – including streets of half-timbered houses and the magnificent cathedral (see pp24–6) – attract thousands of visitors.

2 Abbaye de Jumièges

The remains of this 7th-century abbey (see pp22–3), which housed 900 monks, but was reduced to ruins in the Revolution, are stunning.

3 Giverny

Pay homage to Monet in his own home, the Fondation Claude Monet (see pp40–43), and wander in the garden that inspired him. The Musée des Impressionnismes explores the history of Impressionism and Post-Impressionism.

4 Dieppe

MAP G1 ■ Tourist office: Pont Jehan Ango, Quai du Carénage; 02 32 14 40 60; www.dieppetourisme.com

The first beach resort in France, Dieppe (see p76) occupies a striking position between limestone cliffs. As a Channel port, it was coveted for centuries by foreign invaders, and has long been a favourite with British tourists, for its sweeping beach and lively old town centred on the Grande Rue. Nearby, Église St-Jacques has a memorial to the thousands of Canadians killed in Operation Jubilee in 1942. Above the town, the medieval castle is now a museum, with a fine Impressionist collection and some remarkable 16th-century carved ivory. Dieppe's other engaging museum is the Cité de la Mer, with aquariums and exhibits on maritime history.

Boats moored at Dieppe harbour

5 Le Havre

MAP E2 ■ Tourist office: 186 Blvd Clémenceau; 02 32 74 04 04

Founded in 1517 to replace the silted-up ports of Honfleur, Harfleur and Caudebec, Le Havre is now France's second port and a UNESCO World Heritage Site, a tribute to its recovery from the bombing that flattened it in 1944. One of the few survivors is the 16th-century cathedral, a hybrid of Gothic and Renaissance styles. The city was rebuilt to designs by Auguste Perret, and the starkly imposing Église St-Joseph is typical of his style. More modern is the glass, aluminium and steel structure housing the Musée Malraux (see p55).

6 Côte d'Albâtre
MAP E2, F1, G1, H1

On first sight of the Alabaster Coast, you might think that you were across the Channel: it bears a striking resemblance to the White Cliffs of Dover. Stretching southwest from Le Tréport to Le Havre, the coastline is pitted by *valleuses* – dry hanging valleys in the clifftops, revealed as the cliffs retreat before the combined forces of sea and weather. Harbours shelter in natural shingle inlets, while larger towns cluster on the estuaries. This coast offers some of the region's most spectacular scenery.

Falaise d'Aval as seen from Étretat

7 Étretat

Nestling between two cliffs, Falaises d'Aval and d'Amont, this picturesque village *(see pp30–31)* was a sleepy place until the 19th-century onslaught of writers, painters and Parisian holiday-makers. For the best view of Falaise d'Aval – an extraordinary rock formation with a natural arch – climb to Notre-Dame-de-la-Garde, the mariners' chapel atop Falaise d'Amont. Nearby, a monument commemorates aviators Nungesser and Coli, whose aeroplane was last seen near here on the first, failed attempt to fly across the Atlantic in 1927. In Étretat itself, visit Place Foch, where 16th-century houses cluster around timbered *halles* – an attractive 1920s reconstruction of a covered market – and admire the town's stunning *belle époque* mansions.

THE SEINE

The second-longest, busiest and most famous river in France, the Seine has its source in Burgundy, flows through Paris, and finally meets the sea at Le Havre. Its lower course through Normandy is wide enough to accommodate large ships and barges: hence its historical importance for settlers and invaders, and the location of Rouen and the Norman abbeys.

8 Fécamp
MAP F2 ■ Tourist office: Quai Sadi-Carnot; 02 35 28 51 01

After a casket believed to contain precious drops of Christ's blood was washed ashore in the 1st century, Fécamp became a pilgrimage centre. First an abbey (now ruined) was built to house the holy relic, after which the glorious Abbatiale de la Trinité *(see p52)* was erected in the 12th to 13th centuries. More prosaically, the cornerstone of this no-nonsense fishing port has been the humble cod. Fécamp's other claim to fame is as the birthplace of the herbal liqueur Bénédictine, first concocted in 1863 by merchant Alexandre le Grand, using an old monastic recipe. It continues to be distilled in his overblown 19th-century Gothic Palais Bénédictine *(see p90)*, which contains laboratories, a museum and gallery, and offers tastings.

Palais Bénédictine, Fécamp

Atmospheric Château Gaillard

⑨ Les Andelys and Château Gaillard

MAP H3 ■ Tourist office: 2 Rue Grande; 02 32 21 31 29

The twin villages of Grand and Petit Andelys enjoy a glorious setting on a lazy curve of the Seine in the shadow of the pale ruins of Richard the Lionheart's Château Gaillard, built at break-neck speed in 1196 to prevent Philippe Auguste from reaching Rouen. Below lie the winding streets of tranquil, timbered Petit Andely, and more commercial Grand Andely, with a grand 16th- to 17th-century church and a couple of interesting museums – one dedicated to the painter Nicolas Poussin, the other to the Normandie-Niémen regiment.

⑩ Lyons-la-Forêt

MAP H3 ■ Tourist office: 25 Bis Place Benserade; 02 32 49 31 65

Visit this picture-postcard town in the Lieure Valley and you'll understand why Maurice Ravel used to come here to compose. Sights nearby include the impressive early 17th-century pink-brick Château de Fleury-la-Forêt, with a superb collection of toys and dolls; Château de Vascoeuil, which has traditional cottages and modern sculpture in its grounds; and the ruined Cistercian Abbaye de Mortemer, with its museum.

A DRIVE THROUGH THE VAL DE SEINE

▶ MORNING

Take the D982 from Rouen to St-Martin-de-Boscherville to visit the lovely Romanesque abbey of **St-Georges de Boscherville** (see p88). Walk around the gardens and enjoy the views. After a browse in the abbey shop, revive yourself at one of the village bars.

Continue on the D982 until you reach the D143 turn-off for the bewitching, ruined **Abbaye de Jumièges** (see pp22–3). This is a place for calm contemplation, so don't rush your visit. Afterwards, make your way to the picturesque Seine-side inn **Auberge du Bac** (2 Rue Alphonse Callais) for lunch.

AFTERNOON

From Jumièges, cross over the river by *bac* (ferryboat) into the Forêt de Brotonne (see p63) in the **Parc Naturel Régional des Boucles de la Seine Normande** (see p60). Spend some time exploring this tranquil forest, which has one of the largest concentrations of beech trees in France. Cross the elegant Pont de Brotonne (see p63) over to the town of **Caudebec-en-Caux** (see p88) and admire its splendid Flamboyant Gothic church and medieval Maison des Templiers.

Take the D81 on to the delightful little riverside town of **Villequier** (see p88). Enjoy a walk along the promenade here and watch the boats go by, before heading for dinner at Michelin-starred **Le Manoir de Rétival** (see p91), which also offers stylish accommodation and views of the Seine.

See map on p84 ←

The Best of the Rest

1 Le Tréport
MAP H1 ▪ Tourist office:
Quai Sadi Carnot; 02 35 86 05 69

This popular seaside town is famous
for its smoked fish *(see p90)*, and
also for the view of the coast from the
Calvaire (calvary) above the town.

2 Caudebec-en-Caux
MAP G2 ▪ Tourist office: Pl du
Général de Gaulle; 02 32 70 46 32

A jaunty Seine-side town with a
centuries-old Saturday market, Gothic
church and medieval Templar's house.

3 Villequier
MAP F2 ▪ Musée Victor-Hugo:
02 35 56 78 31; Opening times vary,
call ahead; Adm

Set in a beautiful spot on the Seine,
Villequier marks the point where
river becomes estuary. Victor Hugo's
daughter Léopoldine drowned here
in 1843. The Musée Victor-Hugo
commemorates her life.

4 Abbaye de St-Wandrille
MAP G2 ▪ Guided tours: call
02 35 96 23 11 for details

The chequered history of this working
Benedictine monastery goes back to
649, and even includes a spell as
home to the Marquis of Stackpole
in the 19th century.

5 Varengeville-sur-Mer
MAP G1

Gloriously situated, its clifftop
church has windows by Ubac
and Braques. Lutyens and Jekyll
collaborated on the nearby Parc
du Bois des Moutiers *(see p65)*.

6 Eu
MAP H1 ▪ Tourist office: Pl
Guillaume le Conquérant; www.
destination-letreport-mers.fr

This handsome riverside
town is named after the Irish
Archbishop St Lawrence
(Lorcán Ua – or Eu – Tuathail),
who died here in 1180.

Ruins of the castle in Gisors

7 Gisors
MAP J3 ▪ Tourist office:
1 Passage du Monarque; 02 32
27 60 63 ▪ www.tourisme-gisors.fr

In the capital of Norman Vexin, a
fine 13th- to 14th-century church
keeps company with the imposing
castle, which William the Conqueror
constructed to protect his borders.

8 Écouis
MAP H3 ▪ Abbaye de Fontaine
Guérard: Fleury-sur-Andelle; open
May–Aug: pm Tue–Sun; Adm

At the heart of Écouis is the church
of Notre-Dame, built in 1313. The
nearby ruined 12th-century Abbaye
de Fontaine Guérard is worth a
short excursion.

9 Abbaye St-Georges de Boscherville
MAP G3 ▪ St-Martin-de-
Boscherville ▪ Open Apr–Oct:
9:30am–6:30pm daily; Nov
& Mar: 2–5pm daily ▪ Adm
▪ www.abbayesaintgeorges.fr

This is an exquisite example
of Norman Romanesque
architecture.

Carving at Boscherville

10 Veules-les-Roses
MAP G1 ▪ Tourist office: 27
Rue Victor Hugo; 02 35 97 63 05

In its own valley, at the mouth
of France's shortest river, this
pretty village clusters around
a 12th-century church.

Châteaux

1 ### Château d'Eu
MAP H1 ■ Eu ■ Open mid-May–Oct: 10am–noon & 2–6pm Wed–Mon (Fri pm only) ■ Adm

Queen Victoria came to stay in Louis Philippe's 16th-century holiday home. It is now the Musée Louis-Philippe, crammed with antiques.

2 ### Château de Filières
MAP F2 ■ Gommerville ■ 02 35 20 53 30 ■ Open May, Jun & Sep: 2–6pm Sat, Sun & hols; Jul & Aug: 2–6pm daily ■ Adm

The left wing is all that remains of the original Henri IV house. The park's beech avenue is dubbed La Cathédrale because it resembles Gothic vaults.

3 ### Château de Clères
MAP G2 ■ Clères ■ 02 35 33 23 08 ■ Open Mar, Sep & Oct: 9:30am–12:30pm & 1:30–6:30pm Mon, Tue, Thu & Fri, 10am–6:30pm Wed, Sat & Sun; Apr–Aug:10am–7pm daily ■ Adm

This impressive château has extensive gardens that harbour a small zoo and are open to the public.

4 ### Château de Vascoeuil
MAP H3 ■ Vascoeuil ■ 02 35 23 62 35 ■ Open May–Oct: 10am–6pm daily ■ Adm ■ www.chateau vascoeuil.com

There are more than 60 sculptures throughout the grounds here. It also holds temporary art exhibitions.

5 ### Château d'Ételan
MAP F3 ■ St-Maurice-d'Ételan ■ Opening times vary, check website ■ Adm ■ www.chateau-etelan.fr

A striking example of the 15th-century Flamboyant Gothic, this château has a jewel of a chapel. Book in advance.

6 ### Château de Bizy
MAP H4 ■ Vernon ■ 02 32 51 00 82 ■ Open Jun–Oct: 2–6pm Tue–Sun ■ Adm ■ www.chateaudebizy.com

Book ahead for guided tours of this splendid chateau built in the style of Versailles and once owned by Louis XV.

7 ### Château du Mesnil-Geoffroy
MAP G1 ■ Ermenouville ■ Open May–Sep: 2–6pm Wed–Sun & hols ■ Adm ■ www.chateau-mesnil-geoffroy.com

This 17th-century house of brick and stone has extensive grounds with a wonderful hornbeam maze by Le Nôtre gardener Colinet, a pretty rose garden and a kitchen garden.

8 ### Château de Miromesnil
MAP G1 ■ Tourville-sur-Arques ■ Open mid-May–Oct: 2–6pm Mon–Fri, 10am–6pm Sat & Sun ■ Adm ■ www.chateaumiromesnil.com

Visit the Montebello salon and the Marquis de Miromesnil's rooms at this 16th- to 17th-century mansion where writer Guy de Maupassant was born. The gardens have been classified as a Jardin Remarquable.

Château de Miromesnil

9 ### Manoir d'Ango
MAP G1 ■ Varengeville-sur-Mer ■ 02 35 83 61 56 ■ Open May–Sep: 10am–12:30pm & 2–6pm daily; Oct: Sat, Sun & public hols ■ Adm

Built in the 16th century, this is a glorious Italian Renaissance manor.

10 ### Château d'Orcher
MAP F2 ■ Gonfreville l'Orcher ■ 02 35 45 45 91 ■ Opening times vary, check website ■ Adm ■ www.chateaudorcher.com

This 11th-century fort (remodelled in the 18th century) has a spectacular clifftop setting and a sweeping park with pretty avenues of ash trees.

See map on p84 ←

Places to Shop

① Abbaye de St-Wandrille
MAP G2

A 14th-century barn houses the shop of the famous abbey *(see p88)*. This is the main outlet for the monks' products, including CDs of Gregorian chant, honey, and beeswax candles.

② La Requinque, Rouen
MAP N5 ■ 50 Rue d'Amiens ■ Open 10am–7pm Tue–Sat

This eco-friendly store in Rouen specializes in upcycled goods. Find eye-catching items created by local craftmakers, including quirky vintage lamps, toys, tote bags and canvas pouches.

③ La Chocolatière, Rouen
MAP L5 ■ 18 Rue Guillaume le Conquérant

A haven for chocolate lovers, this sleek grey shop's signature treat is the deliciously decadent Rouen speciality *paillardises* (rich praline-layered chocolates).

④ Manoir de Cateuil
MAP F2 ■ Rte du Havre

This lovely chateau is home to the Ferme Le Valaine, which produces homemade ciders and goat's cheese, as well as tasty ice creams and choco-late made with fresh goat's milk.

⑤ Palais Bénédictine, Fécamp
MAP F2 ■ 110 Rue Alexandre-le-Grand ■ Closed Jan–early Feb

Taste the liqueur, aged in casks in the palace basement, before visiting the shop, well stocked with bottles of Bénédictine and B&B (Bénédictine blended with brandy).

⑥ Pêcheurs d'Islande, Fécamp
MAP F2 ■ 41 Quai Berigny

Dating back to 1872, this seafood delicatessen sells smoked and marinated salmon, mackerel and herring, prawns, and unusual seaweed-based oils and pâtés.

⑦ Caves Bérigny, Rouen
MAP L5 ■ 7 Rue Rollon ■ 02 35 07 57 54 ■ Open 9:30am–7:30pm Tue–Sat, 10am–1pm Sun

French wines and Normandy ciders line the shelves at this attractive shop. There are also branches in Fécamp, Lillebonne and Le Havre.

⑧ L'Epicerie Olivier, Dieppe
MAP G1 ■ 16 Rue St-Jacques ■ 02 35 84 22 55 ■ Open Tue–Sat (Jul & Aug: also Mon pm)

Every kind of French gourmet product is stocked here: charcuterie and cheeses, fine coffees, mustards, spices, oils and preserves. There's also a magnificent selection of fine wines, ciders and liqueurs.

Cheeses at L'Epicerie Olivier, Dieppe

⑨ Maison du Lin, Routot
MAP G3 ■ Pl du Général-Leclerc ■ 02 32 56 21 76 ■ Open Apr–Jun & Sep: 2–6pm Wed–Sun; Jul & Aug: 2–6:30pm Tue–Sun

Learn about the history and production of linen at this museum, then treat yourself to some napkins.

⑩ Saveur Chocolat, Le Havre
MAP F2 ■ 19 Rue Albert André-Huet

The Auzou family have been *chocolatiers* since 1961. Their shop is the place to buy "Tears of Joan of Arc" (chocolate-covered almonds).

Places to Eat

PRICE CATEGORIES
For a three-course meal for one with half
a bottle of wine (or equivalent meal),
taxes and extra charges.

€ under €40   €€ €40–€60   €€€ over €60

1 Gill, Rouen
MAP G3 ▪ 8–9 Quai de la Bourse
▪ 02 35 71 16 14 ▪ €€

Chef Gill Tournadre may have given
up his two Michelin stars, but this
restaurant still produces top-quality
food – albeit at more affordable prices.

**2 La Licorne Royale,
Lyons-la-Forêt**
MAP H3 ▪ 27 Pl Benserade ▪ 02 32 48
24 24 ▪ Closed Wed & Thu ▪ €€€

The restaurant of the Hôtel de la
Licorne creatively combines rustic
charm with modern cuisine.

**3 Au Souper Fin,
Frichemesnil**
MAP H2 ▪ 1 Rte de Clères ▪ 02 35 33
33 88 ▪ Closed Sun D, Tue & Wed ▪ €€€

This snug restaurant is the perfect
place to sample Eric Buisset's
inventive, Michelin-starred cooking.

**4 Le Manoir de Rétival,
Caudebec-en-Caux**
MAP G2 ▪ 2 Rue St-Clair ▪ 06 50 23
43 63 ▪ €€€

Chef David Goërne offers a different
tasting menu every day. Book ahead.

5 Bistrot du Pollet, Dieppe
MAP G1 ▪ 23 Rue Tête-de-
Boeuf ▪ 02 35 84 68 57 ▪ Closed Sun
& Mon ▪ €€

Slightly out of the way, this little
bistro can put fish on your table
minutes after it has been caught.

6 Homard Bleu, Le Tréport
MAP H1 ▪ 45 Quai François 1er
▪ 02 35 86 15 89 ▪ €

Wonderful seafood platters, lobster
and fresh fish are the speciality here.
Book ahead for an upstairs table with
views of the harbour. Excellent service.

Domaine St-Clair, Le Donjon-Étretat

**7 Domaine St-Clair,
Le Donjon-Étretat**
MAP F2 ▪ Chemin de St-Clair
▪ 02 35 27 08 23 ▪ €€

Dine by candlelight at this elegant
Michelin-starred restaurant housed
in a dramatically located seaside
hotel. Chef Gabin Bouguet offers four
fixed-price menus in addition to a
good selection of à la carte dishes.

**8 Le Moulin de Fourges,
Fourges**
MAP J4 ▪ 38 Rue du Moulin ▪ 02 32
52 12 12 ▪ Closed Nov–mid-Mar, Sun
D, Mon & Tue ▪ €€

A pretty mill on the bank of the Epte
offers memorable regional cuisine
in a great setting. Fresh produce is
prepared with skill and imagination.

**9 Restaurant Baudy,
Giverny**
MAP H4 ▪ 81 Rue Claude Monet ▪ 02
32 21 10 03 ▪ Closed Nov–Mar, Sun D
& Mon ▪ €

The classic bistro lunches served
here make a great accompaniment
to any visit to Monet's garden.

10 La Closerie, Vieux Villez
MAP H3 ▪ 17 Rue de l'Église
▪ 02 32 77 44 77 ▪ €

Located in the grounds of the
Château Corneille, La Closerie offers
regional specialities, a wide range
of wines and two creative set menus
based on locally sourced ingredients.

See map on p84 ←

🔟 Central Normandy

Encompassing the whole of the *département* of Calvados and much of Eure, this region is the true heart of Normandy. From the earthly pleasures of Deauville to the heavenly aspirations of St Thérèse's Lisieux, from the rural idyll of the Pays d'Auge to the architectural magnificence of the Château de Beaumesnil, and from the Bayeux Tapestry to the Impressionist paintings inspired by the enchanting seaport of Honfleur, central Normandy is brimming with variety and interest. William the Conqueror – born in Falaise, buried in Caen – dominates the region's history, as do the bloody events of D-Day, 6 June 1944, and the subsequent Battle of Normandy, played out on its wide, sandy beaches and in its attractive, historic and now carefully restored towns.

Exhibit from Musée d'Évreux

CENTRAL NORMANDY

Key	
① Top 10 Sights	**①** Châteaux
see pp93–5	see p96
① Places to Eat	**①** Country Towns
see p99	see p98
① Religious Buildings	
see p97	

1 Caen

MAP D3 ▪ **Tourist office: Pl
St-Pierre; www.caenlamer-tourisme.fr**
Reconstructed after the war, Caen
retains its compact historic centre
and Romanesque masterpieces,
including William the Conqueror's
abbey church of St-Étienne, which
sheltered hundreds of citizens during
the ferocious Battle of Caen in 1944.
Many visitors head straight for the
absorbing Le Mémorial de Caen
(see p54) on the outskirts and then
leave, but it is worth spending time
in this lively, cultured city.

2 Honfleur

The highlight of Normandy's
coast is this enchanting port (see
pp20–21), fortified during the Hundred
Years' War when it was fought over by
the French and the English. Today, it

Honfleur's picturesque harbour

is celebrated for both the mariners
who set sail from its harbour and
the artists who found inspiration
here. The special light of the estuary
is at its best just after dawn.

3 Bayeux

Known the world over for its
famous tapestry (see pp16–19), this
small-scale cathedral town itself is
less well known – yet full of charm.
Allow two hours for a visit to the
tapestry in the Centre Guillaume-le-
Conquérant, and at least another
two hours to explore Vieux Bayeux.

A scene from the Bayeux Tapestry

4 Pays d'Auge

If Normandy's coastline
reaches a peak of loveliness between
Cabourg and Honfleur, then so does
the landscape beyond. This is the
Pays d'Auge (see pp38–9), rich in
orchards and dairy farms, which
stretches back from the coast
through the heart of the département
of Calvados. Lisieux is famed for
its connections with St Thérèse, its
principal town, and there are many
old manors and pretty villages to
explore, too – as well as cheese,
cider and Calvados to taste and buy.

5 D-Day Beaches

Over 70 years after D-Day, the momentous events of 6 June 1944, when the Allies landed on the beaches (see pp34–7) of the Seine Bay, are commemorated in moving memorials, museums and cemeteries.

6 Deauville and La Côte Fleurie

Normandy's most alluring stretch of coast, fringed by marvellous sandy beaches, is enlivened by a string of resorts that offer something for everyone: gambling (or, if you can't afford to gamble, people-watching) in opulent Deauville (see pp32–3); shrimping and sand-yachting in Houlgate and Cabourg; and the many amusements of happy-go-lucky Trouville. The D513 follows the coast, dipping inland around the impressive corniche, Falaises des Vaches Noires, that rises up between Houlgate and Villers-sur-Mer.

Château d'Anet, Vallée de l'Eure

7 Vallée de l'Eure

MAP H4 ■ Tourist office: Pl Dufay, Pacy-sur-Eure; 02 32 26 18 21

Easily accessible from Paris, the lush Eure Valley is a popular weekend destination for city dwellers. The stretch of the Eure between Chartres and the Seine is sometimes referred to as the Valley of the Mistresses, since it passes first the château of Louis XIV's secret wife, Madame de Maintenon (just outside Normandy in Île de France), then Château d'Anet (see p96), commissioned by Diane de Poitiers, mistress of Henri II. From Anet, the D143 and D836 follow the

> **CALVADOS**
>
> The creation of Normandy's famous cider brandy is an art with many subtle variations. Look out on the label for VSOP (four years in the barrel), and Napoléon, Hors d'Age or Age Inconnu (at least five years in the barrel). Drink it as a *digestif*, or follow French tradition and add a splash of *calva* to your coffee. If any excuse will do, knock back a *trou normand* (see p73).

river past Ivry-la-Bataille and Pacy-sur-Eure, with its fine 13th-century church. A lovely stretch at Cocherel comes next, then Château d'Acquigny, set in a park. The Eure ends at Louviers, which has a small but pretty old quarter near its 13th-century church of Notre-Dame (see p97).

8 Évreux

MAP H4 ■ Tourist office: 11 Rue du la Harpe; 02 32 24 04 43

Capital of the *département* of Eure, Évreux has had a turbulent history and more than its fair share of siege and invasion since the Vandals first sacked it in the 5th century. Damaged during World War II, its centre has been rebuilt, with enjoyable gardens and riverside walks. In the Cathédrale de Notre-Dame, Renaissance carvings round the north door date from the height of the Flamboyant period, as do the leaf and flower motifs in the transept and the lantern tower. The Musée d'Évreux includes Gallo-Roman archaeological finds, plus fine medieval misericords and tapestries.

9 Falaise

MAP E4 ■ Tourist office: Pl Guillaume le Conquérant; 02 31 90 17 26; www.falaise-tourisme.com

The equestrian statue of William the Conqueror sets the tone in the main square of this attractive town. Falaise is dominated by the vast Château Guillaume-le-Conquérant, birthplace of William in 1027. In August 1944, it was the site of the fierce and decisive Battle of the Mortain-Falaise Pocket. In the valley below, a modern

Château Guillaume-le-Conquérant

sculpture recalls the spot where William's father, Robert the Magnificent, saw his future wife washing clothes in the stream. Also worth a visit are Automates Avenue, a collection of 20th-century Parisian shop window automata, and Musée André Lemaitre, with a collection dedicated to this famous locally born artist.

⑩ La Suisse Normande

MAP D4–5 ■ Tourist office: 2 Pl St-Sauveur, Thury-Harcourt; 02 31 79 70 45; www.suisse-normande-tourisme.com

This striking region is as close to resembling Switzerland as Normandy gets, and very different from the typical Norman landscape. On its winding northwesterly course, the River Orne has cut through the *massif*, creating steep banks and the occasional peak. None of the "heights" are particularly high, but they provide some dizzying views – and plenty of scope for outdoor pursuits. Many come for the canoeing, walking, fishing or rock-climbing; others to hang-glide off the Pain de Sucre. Another high point is the craggy Roche d'Oëtre, with stunning views over the Rouvre gorges. Thury-Harcourt, Pont-d'Ouilly and Clécy (see p98) are the main centres.

Climbing in La Suisse Normande

A DRIVE ALONG THE RISLE

▶ MORNING

Starting in **Pont-Audemer** (see p98), follow the signposted trail around the town's highlights. On a Friday (market day), Rue de la République is always lined with a tempting array of food stalls.

Take the D130 for the lovely 24-km (15-mile) drive along the Risle and through the Fôret de Montfort to **Le Bec-Hellouin** (see p52). Wander in the abbey grounds and tour the abbey with a monk as your guide. The village (see p57) is a perfect spot for lunch. If you have a picnic, head back to Pont-Authou, just north of Le Bec-Hellouin, and follow signs over a footbridge to Canoe-Kayak-La Risle, a tranquil spot on an island in the river.

AFTERNOON

Leave Le Bec-Hellouin on the scenic D39 to St-Martin-du-Parc and Le Buhot, then turn left on the D26 to **Harcourt**, with its stern medieval fortress-château (see p96) and the oldest arboretum in France. Leaving by the D137, reconnect with the Risle at **Brionne** (see p98). There's plenty to do here, including canoeing or renting a pedalo. The square *donjon* (keep) on its hill is a fine sight against the setting sun and gives a wonderful panoramic view over the Risle Valley.

In town, there's a choice of cafés and restaurants for a relaxing evening drink or a meal. The best is the 18th-century **Auberge du Vieux Donjon** (Rue Soie).

See map on pp92–3 ←

Châteaux

1 Château de Balleroy
MAP C3 ▪ 02 31 21 60 61
▪ Open Easter–Jun, Sep & Oct: Wed–Sun; Jul & Aug: daily ▪ Adm

Portraits of Napoleon and Wellington confront one another in the Waterloo Room of this sumptuous 16th-century château. A fascinating hot-air balloon museum is also housed in the stables.

Château de Beaumesnil and gardens

2 Château de Beaumesnil
MAP G4 ▪ Open May & Jun: pm Sat & Sun; Jul, Aug & Sep: daily ▪ Adm ▪ www.chateaubeaumesnil.com

This Baroque masterpiece, a frothy pile of pink brick and pale stone on a glassy moat, is perfectly complemented by the lovely formal gardens that surround it.

3 Château d'Anet
MAP H4 ▪ Open Apr–Oct: pm Wed–Mon; Feb, Mar & Nov: pm Sat & Sun ▪ Adm ▪ www.chateau-d-anet.com

Now but a glimmer of its former glory, this château still impresses. Make sure you visit the two chapels.

4 Château Saint Germain de Livet
MAP F4 ▪ 02 31 31 00 03 ▪ Open Apr–Oct: Tue–Sun ▪ Adm

Impressive 15th-century brick-and-timber château with its own moat.

5 Château de Crèvecoeur
MAP E4 ▪ Crèvecoeur-en-Auge
▪ Open Apr–Jun & Sep: 11am–6pm daily; Jul & Aug: 11am–7pm daily; Oct: 2–6pm Sat & Sun ▪ Adm ▪ www.chateaudecrevecoeur.com

A castle, reached by a footbridge, survives at the heart of this complex.

6 Château de Champ-de-Bataille, Le Neubourg
MAP G4 ▪ Open Apr–Jun & Sep–Oct: 2–6pm Wed–Sun; Jul & Aug: 2–6:30pm daily ▪ Adm ▪ www.chateauduchampdebataille.com

This 17th-century château is owned by designer Jacques Garcia. On view are the kitchens and lavish gardens.

7 Château de Fontaine-Henry
MAP D3 ▪ Opening times vary, check website ▪ Adm ▪ www.chateaude-fontainehenry.com

The huge sloping roofs of this extraordinary Renaissance château are actually taller than its walls.

8 Le Domaine d'Harcourt
MAP G4 ▪ Open mid-Jun–mid-Sep: daily; Mar–mid-Jun, mid-Sep–mid-Nov: pm Wed–Mon ▪ www.harcourt-normandie.fr

This medieval moated castle is the ancestral home of the Harcourt family, and has an arboretum, created in 1802.

9 Château de Creully
MAP D3 ▪ 02 31 80 18 65
▪ Open Feb–Apr: Mon & Wed–Fri; May–Oct: Mon–Fri ▪ Adm

In the same family since 1613, this château has retained its Louis XIII decoration.

10 Château de Pontécoulant
MAP D4 ▪ 02 31 69 62 54
▪ Open mid-Mar–Apr & Oct–mid-Nov: pm Tue–Sun; May–Sep: 10:30am–noon & 2:30–6pm Tue–Sun ▪ Adm

This 16th- to 18th-century château in the Suisse Normande has long, formal lawns, backed by woodland.

Religious Buildings

1 Abbaye d'Ardenves, Caen
MAP D3

During the Battle of Normandy, 23 Canadian soldiers were executed at this 12th-century abbey on the town's outskirts; a memorial garden commemorates them. The partially ruined church is a fine example of Norman Gothic architecture.

2 Abbaye St-Martin-de-Mondaye, Juaye-Mondaye
MAP D3

The monks of this small community welcome guests on retreat, and host summer concerts in their handsome 18th-century abbey.

3 Prieuré de St-Gabriel, Brécy
MAP D3

Set around a courtyard, the lovely honey-stone buildings of this former daughter house of Le Trinité in Fécamp (see p52) are now occupied by a horticultural school. They can be viewed from the outside only.

4 St-Pierre, Thaon
MAP D3

No longer in use, this striking 12th-century church is a lovely sight in its secluded setting, hidden by greenery at the tip of a valley. A real gem of Romanesque architecture.

5 Église Abbatiale, St-Pierre-sur-Dives
MAP E4

The copper strip on the nave's floor shows the position of the sun's rays at this large church, once part of an abbey (see p38).

St-Pierre-sur-Dives

6 Ste-Foy, Conches-en-Ouche
MAP G4

This Flamboyant Gothic church (see p98) has some of the finest stained glass in Normandy. Its spire is a copy of one destroyed in a storm in 1842.

7 Abbaye-aux-Hommes, Caen
MAP L2

This Romanesque abbey (see p53) was built by William the Conqueror. Guided tours reveal the rest of the abbey complex, including the lovely cloister.

Abbaye-aux-Hommes, Caen

8 Abbaye Notre-Dame, Le Bec-Hellouin
MAP G3

There is a marvellous view of the abbey (see p52) as you enter the village from the south. The refectory has been converted into a simple church, where its founder lies buried beneath the altar.

9 Notre-Dame, Louviers
MAP H3

From the 13th century, Louviers was an important centre of cloth-making. Its lavishly decorated church reflects the town's former prosperity.

10 Notre-Dame, Verneuil-sur-Avre
MAP G5

Built of a reddish stone called grison, this church is noted for its plethora of 16th-century statues (see p98).

See map on pp92–3

Country Towns

Ruins at Beaumont-le-Roger

(1) Beaumont-le-Roger
MAP G4 ▪ Tourist office: 6 Pl de l'Eglise; 02 32 44 05 79

The stark ruins of the 13th-century priory and the parish church of St-Nicolas are the main sights in this riverside town.

(2) Bernay
MAP F4 ▪ Tourist office: 29 Rue Thiers; 02 32 43 32 08

The town of Bernay has some picturesque timbered houses (look for Rue Gaston-Follope, lined with antiques shops), a museum, and an abbey church begun in 1013.

(3) Brionne
MAP G3 ▪ Tourist office: 1 Rue du Général-de-Gaulle; 02 32 44 05 79

An excellent base for exploring the Risle Valley, this small market town is overlooked by an 11th-century keep.

(4) Clécy
MAP D4 ▪ Tourist office: Pl du Tripot; 02 31 79 70 45

This pretty, stone-built village in La Suisse Normande (see p95) features a model railway (see p68) and a range of holiday activities.

(5) Conches-en-Ouche
MAP G4 ▪ Tourist office: Pl Briand; 02 32 30 76 42

Set above a bend in the River Rouloir, Conches has a number of medieval houses and a church that is home to some fine stained-glass windows.

(6) Orbec
MAP F4 ▪ Tourist office: 6 Rue Grande; 02 31 48 18 10

This delightful country town has many fine old buildings, including the 1563 Vieux Manoir in Rue Grande.

(7) Pont-Audemer
MAP F3 ▪ Tourist office: Pl du Gén de Gaulle; 02 32 41 08 21

Amid nondescript surroundings, Pont-Audemer's charming centre is filled with half-timbered houses.

(8) Verneuil-sur-Avre
MAP G5 ▪ Tourist office: 129 Pl de la Madeleine; 02 32 32 17 17

This town on the old Franco-Norman border is famous for the chequered brickwork of its buildings, the 13th-century Tour Grise, and the striking tower of Église de la Madeleine.

(9) Beuvron-en-Auge
MAP E3 ▪ Tourist office: 2 Esplanade Woolsery ▪ 02 31 39 59 14

Arguably the prettiest village in the Pays d'Auge (see p38), Beuvron-en-Auge is full of half-timbered houses, gift shops and good restaurants.

(10) Cormeilles
MAP F3 ▪ Tourist office: 21 Pl du Général de Gaulle; 02 32 56 02 39

Cormeilles suffered relatively little war damage. It has a Friday market and a great Calvados distillery (see p39).

A historic street in Cormeilles

Places to Eat

PRICE CATEGORIES
For a three-course meal for one with
half a bottle of wine (or equivalent meal),
taxes and extra charges.

€ under €40   €€ €40–€60   €€€ over €60

① Ivan Vautier, Caen
MAP D3 ▪ 3 Ave Henry Chéron
▪ 02 31 73 32 71 ▪ Closed Sun D,
Mon, 3 weeks Aug ▪ €€€

Ivan Vautier has a Michelin star for
his innovative take on Norman dishes
such as baked pigeon and *tartare de
langoustine* (langoustine tartare).

② Au P'tit Bistrot, Bayeux
MAP D3 ▪ 31 Ter Rue Larcher
▪ 02 31 92 30 08 ▪ Closed Sun & Mon
▪ €€

Just a stone's throw from the
cathedral, this welcoming restaurant
offers a choice menu of well-prepared
seasonal cuisine.

③ Auberge des Deux Tonneaux, Pierrefitte-en-Auge
MAP E3 ▪ Le Bourg ▪ 02 31 64 09 31
▪ Closed Mon D, Tue (except Jul &
Aug) ▪ €

Gorgeous views and traditional
country fare such as suckling pig can
be enjoyed at this 17th-century inn.

④ Au P'tit Normand, Cambremer-en-Auge
MAP E4 ▪ Pl de l'Église ▪ 02 31 32
03 20 ▪ Closed Sun D, Mon, Jan–mid-
Feb ▪ €

This snug bistro is a local favourite
for homemade terrines, mixed
salads and Norman classics.

⑤ Belle Île-sur-Risle, Pont-Audemer
MAP F3 ▪ 112 Rte de Rouen ▪ 02 32
56 96 22 ▪ Closed mid-Nov–Mar ▪ €€

A romantic private island provides
the setting for this elegant mansion
hotel and restaurant. The *pastilla
de lapin* (rabbit in filo pastry) here
is wonderful.

⑥ Les Vapeurs, Trouville
MAP E3 ▪ 160–162 Quai Fernand
Moureaux ▪ 02 31 88 15 24 ▪ €

Fabulous *moules frîtes*, desserts
with lashings of *crème fraîche*
and crisp white wines ensure this
place is always extremely busy.

Popular restaurant Les Vapeurs

⑦ Le Bréard, Honfleur
MAP F3 ▪ 7 Rue du Puits
▪ 02 31 89 53 40 ▪ Closed Mon L, Wed
& Thu (Jul & Sep: open daily, D) ▪ €€

This elegant restaurant specializes
in beautifully presented gourmet
dishes made from local ingredients.

⑧ Le Bistrot d'à Côté, Port-en-Bessin
MAP C3 ▪ 12 Rue Michel Lefournier
▪ 02 31 51 79 12 ▪ Closed Sun–Mon
(Jul & Aug: Mon) ▪ €

The blue-and-white decor befits the
harbourside setting of this bistro.
The seafood is deliciously fresh.

⑨ La Ferme de la Haute Crémonville, St-Étienne-du-Vauvray
MAP H3 ▪ Rte de Crémonville ▪ 02 32
59 14 22 ▪ Closed Wed D, Sat L, Sun ▪ €€

Set in a traditional farmhouse, this
place dishes up tasty local cuisine.

⑩ La Fine Fourchette, Falaise
MAP E4 ▪ 52 Rue Georges
Clemenceau ▪ 02 31 90 08 59
▪ Closed 2 weeks Feb ▪ €€

Just outside Falaise, this place serves
Norman dishes with a refined twist.

See map on pp92–3 ←

TOP10 Northwestern Normandy

Normandy's northwest is a world of its own. Thrusting into the English Channel is the Cotentin Peninsula, with picturesque little ports, long, unspoiled beaches, and gannets and shearwaters wheeling in the sky above wild and windblown headlands. Cotentin's proud maritime heritage is evident, especially in the important strategic port and naval base of Cherbourg, and it was from here in the Middle Ages that the descendants of Norse settlers set sail to establish kingdoms in Sicily and southern Italy. Further south, in the heart of the region – which encompasses the *département* of Manche – lies the marshy landscape of the Marais du Cotentin et du Bessin, a paradise for nature lovers. Further south, there are meadows and hedgerows *(bocage)*, and the lovely River Vire, seemingly made for pleasure.

Painted carving at Coutances cathedral

NORTHWESTERN NORMANDY

Rosslare
Poole, Portsmouth

La Hague Peninsula
Cherbourg-Maupertus
Barfleur
Cherbourg
St-Vaast-la-Hougue
Flamanville
Valognes
Les Pieux
Utah Beach
Bricquebec
Négreville
St-Sauveur-le-Vicomte
Ste-Mère-Église
Barneville-Carteret
Portbail
Omaha Beach
Parc Régional des Marais du Cotentin
Carentan
Colleville-sur-Mer
Laby'parc Maze
Isigny-sur-Mer
Bayeux
Lessay
St-Jean-de-Daye
Tournières
Périers
Marchésieux
Tilly-sur-Seulles
Gouville-sur-Mer
St-Lô
CALVADOS
Gratot
La Vacquerie
Coutances
Vallée de la Vire
Villers-Bocage
Montmartin-sur-Mer
MANCHE
La Ferrière-Harang
Trelly
Abbaye de Hambye
Percy
Campeaux
Le Bény-Bocage
Îles Chausey
Bréhal
Vire
Vassy
Granville
Villedieu-les-Poêles
La Haye-Pesnel

1	Top 10 Sights see pp103–5
1	Places to Eat see p109
1	The Best of the Rest see p106
1	Highlights of the Cotentin Coast see p107
1	Family Outings see p108

0 km   10
0 miles   10

Previous pages Granville's upper town

1 Utah Beach
MAP B3

On D-Day, 6 June 1944, the eastern coast of the Cotentin Peninsula, codenamed Utah Beach *(see pp34–7)*, received thousands of American troops, backed up by paratroopers that were dropped inland around Ste-Mère-Eglise.

2 Cherbourg
MAP B2 ■ Tourist office: 2 Quai Alexandre III; www.encotentin.fr

There's more to Cherbourg, or to give it its full name, Cherbourg-en-Cotentin, than meets the eye. Of particular note is La Cité de la Mer *(see p54)*, which is Europe's deepest aquarium. For a good view of the port, drive to the hilltop Fort du Roule, which houses the Musée de la Libération, recalling the events leading to Cherbourg's liberation on 27 June 1944. Most activity is centred on the market square, Pl Général-de-Gaulle, and along shopping streets such as Rue Tour-Carrée and Rue de la Paix. The town's collection of fine art in the Musée Thomas-Henry (open mid-Mar–Dec) includes portraits by Jean-François Millet *(see p48)*. There's also the interesting Musée d'Histoire Naturelle.

3 La Hague Peninsula
MAP A2 ■ Tourist office: 1 Pl de la Madeleine, Beaumont-Hague; 02 33 52 74 94

Calm and lovely on a sunny spring day, rugged and windswept during a winter storm, this furthest prong of Cotentin is stunningly beautiful. Its stone villages, majestic cliffs, jagged rocks and hidden coves are more reminiscent of Brittany than Normandy, and the presence of a vast nuclear power station in the middle does not detract – at least not too much – from the glorious coastline *(see p105)*.

Lessay's compact abbey church

4 Lessay
MAP B3 ■ Tourist office: 11 Pl St-Cloud; 02 33 45 14 34

The simple, comforting lines of Lessay's abbey church, St-Trinité, make it one of the most beautiful Romanesque buildings in Normandy. Dating from 1098, it was almost destroyed in 1944, but has been magnificently reconstructed using original materials. The interior is plain and lovely, with fine stained glass adding warmth. Sleepy Lessay is also known for its convivial three-day Foire de Sainte-Croix *(see p81)*, an ancient agricultural fair which usually takes place in September.

The rugged Hague Peninsula

5 Villedieu-les-Poêles

MAP B5 ■ Tourist office: 8 Pl des Costils; www.ot-villedieu.fr

Since the 13th century, this little town has been the capital of copper – pots and pans are on sale everywhere. In the Atelier de Cuivre, you can see craftsmen at work, while the atmospheric Fonderie des Cloches gives an insight into the making of bells (clay, horse dung and goat hair are a few components). Another local craft, lacemaking, is covered in the Maison de la Dentellière.

6 Coutances

MAP B4 ■ Tourist office: 6 Rue Milon; www.tourisme-coutances.fr

This isolated corner of France is home to a great cathedral: a soaring stone rocket crowning the hill around which the town of Coutances clusters. In the 13th century, a new Norman Gothic cathedral was built on the remains of the previous, fire-damaged Romanesque one. Its remarkable octagonal lantern rises to 41 m (135 ft), and its many towers, spires and pointed arches sweep the eye skywards. In town, the flower-filled Jardin des Plantes makes a perfect setting for some of the concerts that take place during May's Jazz sous les Pommiers festival *(see p80)*.

Notre-Dame cathedral, Coutances

LE BOCAGE

A rolling landscape of mixed woodland and meadow, bordered by banks topped with high, thick hedgerows, and bisected by narrow, sunken lanes – this is the *bocage* that covers much of Normandy, particularly around St-Lô and Vire. Pastoral in peacetime, it proved a nightmare for the Allies in 1944, making progress against the enemy near impossible.

Abbaye de Hambye's roofless chancel

7 Abbaye de Hambye

MAP B4 ■ Open Apr–Sep: 10am–noon & 2–6pm Wed–Mon; Jul & Aug: 10am–6pm daily ■ Adm

Tucked beneath a wooded escarpment by the River Sienne, Hambye's roofless remains have an immediately calming effect on visitors. The restored monastic buildings of this 12th-century Benedictine abbey now host exhibitions and concerts.

8 Vallée de la Vire

MAP C4 ■ Tourist office: 60 Rue de la Poterne, Saint-Lô; 02 14 29 00 17

As it winds towards the sea, the River Vire cuts through granite schists, forming a ribbon of water amid glorious countryside. Towpaths border most of the river between Vire and St-Lô, so you can picnic, cycle, walk or horse-ride alongside. Condé-sur-Vire is the place for canoeing, while at Roches de Ham, an 80-m (260-ft) rock face towers above the river, offering magnificent views of the valley. It is also home to a welcome crêperie and cider bar in summer. Nearby, the grand chapel at the village of La Chapelle-sur-Vire has been a place of pilgrimage since the 12th century. At Torigni-sur-Vire, the Château des Matignon houses a fine collection of tapestries.

⑨ Granville
MAP B5 ▪ **Tourist office: 2 Rue Lecampion; 02 33 91 30 03**

At first sight, Granville seems an unlikely setting for one of Normandy's most popular seaside resorts (see p67). Ramparts enclose the upper town, which sits on a rocky spur overlooking the Baie du Mont-St-Michel. The town developed from the fortifications built by the English in 1439 as part of their assault on the Mont. In the gatehouse, the Musée d'Art et d'Histoire de Granville recounts Granville's long seafaring tradition. The lower town is the resort, with a casino, promenades and public gardens. From the port, boat trips run to the Îles Chausey.

⑩ Parc Régional des Marais du Cotentin
MAP B3 ▪ **Espace de Découverte: Les Ponts d'Ouve, St-Côme-du-Mont; 02 33 71 65 30; www.parc-cotentin-bessin.fr**

The band of low-lying marshes and water meadows stretching across the base of the Cotentin Peninsula forms a regional park, with rich birdlife, plus houses made from clay and straw. Carentan is the gateway town, with a reception centre at Les Ponts d'Ouve on the D913, in the midst of a watery landscape. Visitors can explore on foot or by boat.

Parc Régional des Marais du Cotentin

A DAY IN COTENTIN

▶ MORNING

Leave Cherbourg on the D901 toward **St-Pierre-Église**. After 15 km (9 miles), turn onto the D355 to pretty **Le Vast** in the heart of the lovely **Val de Saire**. Stop to buy a *brioche du Vast* from La Brioche du Vast (12 les Moulins). Follow the river on the D25 to **Valcanville**, then on the D125 to **La Pernelle**, climbing the steep granite hill to the church and a magnificent panorama of the coast.

In **St-Vaast-la-Hougue** (see p106) stop for a delicious seafood lunch at local favourite **La Bisquine** (33 Quai Vauban), then stock up on food and wine at the family-run emporium **Gosselin**, trading since 1889. If there's time, take a trip to **Île de Tatihou**, just offshore (see p106).

AFTERNOON

From St-Vaast, it's a quick drive along the D14 to **Quineville**, then the coastal D421 to **Utah Beach** to contemplate the events of June 1944 (see pp34–7). After a bracing walk along the beach and dunes, head inland to **Ste-Mère-Église** (see p106) and its church, perhaps pausing for refreshments at Brasserie la Libération on Rue Général-de-Gaulle.

From Ste-Mère-Église, drive into the watery heart of the Cotentin marshlands, ending the day on the banks of the Douve at **Les Moitiers-en-Bauptois**.

See map on p102 ←

The Best of the Rest

1 Valognes
MAP B2 ■ Tourist office:
25 Rue de l'Eglise ■ 02 33 40 11 55
Though badly damaged in 1944,
Valognes retains traces of its glory
days as the "Versailles of the North",
including the Hôtel de Beaumont,
a splendid 18th-century mansion.

2 Portbail
MAP A3 ■ Tourist office: 26
Rue Philippe Lebel; 02 33 04 03 07
A lovely village with access to two
fine beaches. In summer, it hosts
an excellent market every Tuesday.

3 Barneville-Carteret
MAP A3 ■ Tourist office:
3 Ave de la République;
02 33 04 90 58
This lively resort comprises the
villages of Barneville, Carteret and
Barneville-Plage (see p66). Its rocky
headland, Cap de Carteret, makes
for a bracing coastal walk.

4 St-Sauveur-le-Vicomte
MAP B3 ■ 02 33 21 50 44
■ Museum: open Apr–Oct: 2–6pm
Wed–Sun ■ Adm
The 12th-century castle houses the
Musée Barbey-d'Aurevilly, dedicated
to the 19th-century novelist (see p50)
who was born in the town.

5 St-Vaast-la-Hougue and Île de Tatihou
MAP B2 ■ Tourist office: 1 Pl Général-
de-Gaulle; 02 33 71 99 71
The harbour of this small port was
fortified after the French defeat in
1692, as was the Île de Tatihou – now
the site of a garden, bird-watching
post and maritime museum.

6 Abbaye de Cérisy-la-Fôret
MAP C3 ■ Open Apr–Jun & Oct:
2–6pm Tue–Sun; Jul–Sep: 11am–
6pm daily ■ Adm
This Benedictine abbey was founded in
1032 by Duke Robert the Magnificent.
The ruins of the huge nave recall the
monastery's former importance.

7 St-Lô
MAP C4 ■ Tourist office: 60
Rue de la Poterne; 02 14 29 00 17
The regional capital suffered severe
war damage, as testified by its many
memorials and striking half-restored
cathedral. The Musée des Beaux-Arts
displays some great works of art.

8 Château de Gratot
MAP B4 ■ Open daily ■ Adm
■ www.chateaugratot.com
The roofless remains of this once-
great château lie in quiet countryside.
An exhibition tells its story.

9 Ste-Mère-Église
MAP B3 ■ Tourist office:
Rue Eisenhower; 02 33 21 00 33
The church here was made famous
by the film *The Longest Day*. The
Ferme Musée du Cotentin gives an
insight into early 1900s rural life.
There is also a World War II museum.

10 Château de Pirou
MAP B4 ■ Opening times
vary, check website ■ Adm ■ www.
chateau-pirou.fr
Set on an island in the middle of
an artificial lake, this remote 12th-
century fortress is a stirring sight.

Île de Tatihou

Highlights of the Cotentin Coast

Wild Val de Saire coastline

1 Val de Saire
MAP B2

The gentle, verdant valley *(see p71)* east of Barfleur is in sharp contrast to the wild coastline.

2 Querqueville
MAP A2

Beside the hilltop church, and surrounded by a cemetery packed with ornate marble tombs, stands 10th-century St-Germain, the oldest chapel in western France.

3 Château de Nacqueville
MAP A2 ■ Open May–Sep: noon–5pm Thu, Fri, Sun & public hols ■ Adm ■ www.nacqueville.com

The park of this 16th-century château, with its romantic turreted gatehouse, is loveliest in May and June when the rhododendrons are in bloom.

4 Gruchy
MAP A2

This tiny seaside village includes the humble birthplace of Jean-François Millet *(see p48)*, open to the public in summer. Walk to the dramatic Rocher du Castel-Vendon; Millet's painting of it can be seen in the Musée Thomas-Henry in Cherbourg *(see p103)*.

5 Port Racine
MAP A2

En route to Cap de la Hague, France's smallest port is tucked beneath the road. From here, follow signs to Jardins Prévert, an oasis at the head of a wild valley.

6 Îles Chausey
MAP A4

This is a collection of tiny islands and islets in the Channel. The largest, Grande Île, has sweeping sandy beaches and just one hotel. In summer it attracts day-trippers from Granville, an hour's boat ride away.

7 Omonville-la-Petite
MAP A2

The churchyard here contains the uncarved headstone of poet Jacques Prévert, and the graves of his wife and daughter. Nearby is his house *(see p51)*.

8 Barfleur
MAP B2

It is said that William the Conqueror's invasion vessel was built in this fishing port *(see p56)*. Its lighthouse, at Gatteville, is one of the tallest in France, with 365 steps; the reward for climbing up is a fine panorama.

Boats moored in low tide at Barfleur

9 Vauville
MAP A2

The twin attractions here are the subtropical gardens of Château de Vauville and a fine beach that is perfect for sand yachting *(see p68)*.

10 Nez de Jobourg
MAP A2

The desolate Baie d'Ecalgrain sweeps round to this impressive promontory. From here, the road to Vauville is dominated by the Usine Atomique de la Hague nuclear power station.

See map on p102 ←

Family Outings

1 L'Attelage des Grandes Marées, Gouville-sur-Mer

MAP B4 ▪ Booking essential: tourist office; 1 Rue du Nord; 02 33 47 84 33

You can visit this oyster park at low tide in a horse-drawn carriage.

Exhibits at La Cité de la Mer

2 La Cité de la Mer, Cherbourg

Humanity's conquest of the deep is the theme of Cherbourg's former Gare Maritime Transatlantique (see p54). No children under 6 permitted.

3 Train Rides

Train du Cotentin: MAP A3; 02 33 04 70 08 ▪ Mini-train des Marais: MAP C3–B3; 02 14 15 54 91

Take a ride on the Train Touristique du Cotentin along the coast from Carteret to Portbail, or a miniature train through the marshland from Saint Martin d'Aubigny to Periers.

4 Laby'parc Maze

MAP D3 ▪ Rte de Crouay ▪ 06 17 37 45 88 ▪ Open Jul & Aug: 10:30am–7pm daily ▪ Adm

Wander around this delightful giant maze and discover local tales in the heart of the field.

5 Watersports

Jolie France: 02 33 50 31 81; vedettesjoliefrance.com ▪ Cherbourg: www.encotentin.fr

The Jolie France sails from Granville to Chausey's Grand Île (see p107). Cherbourg offers a range of activities, from kayaking to pleasure cruises.

6 Île de Tatihou

Children enjoy the amphibious craft that crosses to this tiny pleasure island with a fascinating history. It is just off St-Vaast-la-Hougue (see p106).

7 Musée du Bocage Normand

MAP C4 ▪ Blvd de la Commune, St-Lô ▪ 02 33 56 26 98 ▪ Open Apr–Jun, Sep & Oct: 2–6pm Tue–Sun; Jul & Aug: 10am–noon & 2–6pm Tue–Sun ▪ Adm

An absorbing museum located in old farm buildings. It shows how the region was farmed in centuries gone by, with plenty of interactive exhibits and reconstructions.

8 Ferme aux 5 Saisons, Flamanville

MAP A2 ▪ 02 33 04 56 84 ▪ Open Jul & Aug: pm Mon–Fri ▪ Adm

A farm for children: see an apple press in action, visit the animals and bake bread for tea.

9 Vélorail, Vallée de la Vire

MAP C4 ▪ Condé-sur-Vire ▪ 02 33 05 46 55 ▪ Open Jul & Aug: daily; mid-Apr–Jun & Sep: Sat, Sun, public hols ▪ www.velorail-normandie.fr

Ride the area's disused railways in a pedal-powered buggy.

10 Musée Christian Dior

MAP B5 ▪ Les Rhumbs, Granville ▪ Open mid-Apr–Sep: daily ▪ Adm ▪ www.musee-dior-granville.com

This exhibition of designs by Dior and other top couturiers is set in his picturesque childhood home.

Musée Christian Dior

Places to Eat

PRICE CATEGORIES

For a three-course meal for one with half a bottle of wine (or equivalent meal), taxes and extra charges.

€ under €40   €€ €40–€60   €€€ over €60

1 Bistro Bouche, Cherbourg

MAP B2 ▪ 25 Tour Carrée ▪ 02 33 04 25 04 ▪ Closed Mon L ▪ €

A cosy interior, charming service and simple but well-cooked classic French dishes ensure that this little bistro is always full with locals and visitors alike.

2 Le Moulin à Vent, St-Germain-des-Vaux

MAP A2 ▪ Hameau Danneville ▪ 02 33 52 75 20 ▪ Closed Fri & Sat L ▪ €€€

Enjoy glorious views and very fresh seafood at very reasonable prices.

3 La Marine, Barneville-Carteret

MAP A3 ▪ 11 Rue de Paris ▪ 02 33 53 83 31 ▪ Open Sep–Jun: Wed–Sun; Jul & Aug: Tue–Sun ▪ €€

The dishes at this hotel restaurant with harbour views range from French classics such as duck foie gras to the more modern such as pollack with creamed turnips, pak choi, whelks and seaweed.

4 Ferme de Malte, Villedieu-les-Poêles

MAP B5 ▪ 11 Rue Tétrel ▪ 02 33 91 35 91 ▪ Closed Wed & Sun D, Mon ▪ €€

Owned by the Knights of Malta, who have a long connection with the town, this smart restaurant specializes in fish, and has two dining rooms.

5 Verte Campagne, Trelly

MAP B4 ▪ 02 33 47 65 33 ▪ Closed Wed ▪ €

A wide enough range of menus to suit most pockets is available at this elegant restaurant in a rustic, ivy-covered farmhouse (see p130).

6 Auberge des Grottes

MAP E4 ▪ 8 Rue des Falaises ▪ 02 33 52 71 44 ▪ Closed Tue D (Sep–Jun), Wed ▪ €

Situated at the very tip of Cap de la Hague, this restaurant offers superb views. The seafood choices are great.

7 La Plancha, Agon-Coutainville

MAP B4 ▪ 77 Rue Dramard ▪ 02 33 47 26 77 ▪ Closed Tue & Wed (Sep–Jun), mid-Nov–mid-Dec ▪ €

This trendy beach brasserie has sea views and an original menu of fresh seafood and fish platters, plus tapas.

8 La Bohème, Barfleur

MAP B2 ▪ 1 Rue Saint-Thomas Becket ▪ 02 14 14 43 18 ▪ Closed Mon ▪ €

La Bohème offers excellent galettes and crêpes. There are views over the harbour and an outside terrace.

La Ferme des Mares

9 La Ferme des Mares, Saint-Germain-sur-Ay

MAP B3 ▪ 02 33 17 01 02 ▪ Closed Mon–Sat L, Sun D ▪ €

This restaurant, once a fortified Norman farm, serves the best local fish, lamb and traditional cheeses.

10 L'Auberge, Mesnil-Rogues

MAP B4 ▪ 02 33 61 37 12 ▪ Opening times vary, call ahead ▪ €

Hams and legs of lamb are spit-roasted at this cosy *auberge*. The fish dishes are also excellent.

See map on p102

🔟 Southern Normandy

From the astonishing sight of Mont-St-Michel, appearing like a fabulous mirage out of the pancake-flat landscape that surrounds it, to the equine elegance of the national stud at Haras du Pin or the human charm of romantic Château d'O, this region, which consists of the *département* of Orne and the southern part of Manche, is crammed with history and variety. The scenery is just as varied: there's the rugged beauty of the Pays d'Alençon in the

Parc Régional de Normandie-Maine, where bands of thick forest cover the high ridges; the wooded Mortainais, with its steep valleys and thrilling waterfalls; the gently rolling pastureland of La Perche, interrupted by cool, deep forests; the narrow lanes and pretty, flower-filled villages of the Pays du Bocage Ornais; and the flat salt marshes of the Baie de Mont-St-Michel.

Mont-St-Michel manuscript, Scriptorial d'Avranches

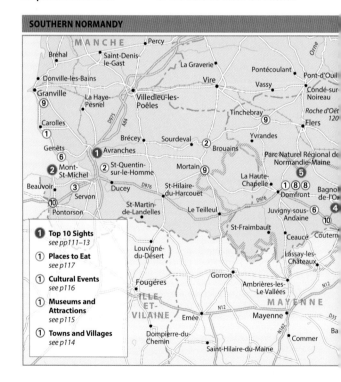

SOUTHERN NORMANDY

1 **Top 10 Sights**
  see pp111–13

1 **Places to Eat**
  see p117

1 **Cultural Events**
  see p116

1 **Museums and Attractions**
  see p115

1 **Towns and Villages**
  see p114

1 Avranches

MAP B5 ■ Tourist office: 2 Rue du Général de Gaulle ■ 02 33 58 00 22

Avranches has a long and historic association with Mont-St-Michel (see pp12–15), which it overlooks across the bay (one of the best views is from the Jardin des Plantes). St Aubert, who founded the abbey there, was Bishop of Avranches; his skull, complete with the hole made by St Michael's finger, is on display in the Basilique de St-Gervais et St-Protais. In an annexe of the former episcopal palace, the Musée d'Avranches contains wonderful collections of medieval sculpture and religious art, and in the Scriptorial d'Avranches you can see the Mont-St-Michel manuscripts, dating back to the 8th century.

St Aubert's skull, Avranches

2 Mont-St-Michel

Despite being the most photographed sight in France, the ethereal beauty of this vast abbey (see pp12–15) can still take your breath away.

3 Alençon

MAP E6 ■ Tourist office: Maison d'Ozé, Pl de la Magdeleine; www.visitalencon.com

This handsome town was a famous lacemaking centre in the 17th and 18th centuries. Examples are displayed in the Musée des Beaux-Arts et de la Dentelle, which presents a history of the industry alongside paintings and Cambodian artifacts. The intricate stonework on the façade of the Église de Notre-Dame even resembles lace; inside, there's a chapel to Alençon-born St Thérèse.

4 Bagnoles-de-l'Orne

MAP D5 ▪ Tourist office: Pl du Marché; www.bagnolesdelorne.com

Clamber to the top of the Roc au Chien for a panorama of this refined spa town steeped in legend *(see p66)*. Its lake, casino, park and avenues of chic houses were built for the wealthy who came to take the waters in the late 19th century. Ailing visitors still flock to the Établissement Thermal, in its striking *belle époque* building.

5 Parc Naturel Régional de Normandie-Maine

MAP D5–E5 ▪ Maison du Parc: Carrouges ▪ 02 33 81 75 75 ▪ Open Apr–Jun & Sep–mid Oct: 10am–noon & 2–6pm daily; Jul & Aug: 10am–12:30pm & 2–6:30pm daily

With a landscape marked by escarpments and forests in the *haut pays* of the Alpes Mancelles, and by rolling hills, *bocage* and open country in the *bas pays* at Saosnois and around Alençon and Sées, this vast natural park *(see p60)* dips south to the Pays-de-Loire. Pick up maps and itineraries at the Maison du Parc in Carrouges. Nature centres are scattered through the park.

6 Le Perche

MAP G6–H6 ▪ Manoir de Courboyer, Nocé; www.parc-naturel-perche.fr

Still relatively unknown, this area is famous for its Percheron horses and its manors. Perche manors are quite different from typical half-timbered Norman farm-houses; they are defensive buildings, made of stone and embellished with turrets and towers. The surrounding countryside is gentle, with undulating hills, dense forest and lush valleys. Grazing Percherons (draughthorses from the

The stately Haras National du Pin

Le Perche's Manoir de Courboyer

region) add an air of serenity. Chief among Perche's villages and towns are Mortagne and Bellême *(see p114)*.

7 Haras National du Pin

MAP E5 ▪ Le Pin-au-Haras ▪ 02 33 36 68 68 ▪ Opening times vary, check website ▪ Tours every half hour ▪ Adm ▪ www.haras-national-du-pin.com

You don't have to be a horse lover to be impressed by the style and splendour of the national stud, a "Versailles for horses" founded by Colbert in the mid-17th century with the approval of the Sun King himself. Colbert commissioned Pierre Le Mousseux to design it. At the end of a long, grassy ride through the surrounding woods, the main château and two elegant former stable blocks enclose a horseshoe-shaped court-yard (Colbert's Court), scene of horse and carriage displays on Thursday afternoons in summer. Tours visit the forge, tack room and stables, where some 100 stallions are kept at stud.

⑧ Château d'O

MAP E5 ▪ Mortrée ▪ 02 33
67 12 48 ▪ Opening times vary: call
the Argentan tourist office for details

With fairy-tale turrets and steep
roofs reflected in the limpid, green
waters of its moat, this early
Renaissance château is utterly
enchanting. It was largely built
during the 15th and 16th centuries,
with a west wing – now the living
quarters – added in the 18th. You
can wander in the grounds or take
a tour of the interior, furnished in
mainly 18th-century style.

Château d'O, Mortrée

⑨ Château de Carrouges

MAP E6 ▪ 02 33 27 20 32
▪ Open Sep–Apr: 10am–12:30pm
& 2–4:30pm daily; May–Aug: 10am–
12:45pm & 2–5:30pm daily ▪ Adm

Until it was bought by the state
in 1936, this imposing château (see
p116) had been in the Le Veneur de
Tillières family for almost 500 years.
Founded by Jean de Carrouges in
the 14th century, it has all the attri-
butes of a grand château: moats,
terraces, gardens, and an elegant
16th-century gatehouse.

⑩ Alpes Mancelles

MAP E6 ▪ Tourist office: 19 Ave
du Docteur Riant, Fresnay-sur-Sarthe;
www.tourisme-alpesmancelles.fr;
closed Mon

In the Parc Naturel Régional de
Normandie-Maine, on Normandy's
southern border, is this rugged landscape of valleys and forests. Mont des
Avaloirs, at 417 m (1,368 ft), is the
joint highest peak in western France.
Of the area's lovely villages, the jewel
is St-Céneri-le-Gérei (see p114).

EXPLORING THE PERCHE

▶ **MORNING**

Pick up a "Circuit du Patrimoine"
from the tourist office in the old
market in **Mortagne-au-Perche**
(pl du Général-de-Gaulle), and
walk its route (see p114), popping
into the Église de Notre-Dame
to see the glorious altarpiece.
Finish with a coffee in the **Hôtel
Tribunal** (see p117).

Leave Mortagne-au-Perche on
the D931 towards Mamers. Turn
left on the D275 and follow signs
to **La Perrière**, an enchanting
village of colourful cottages and
tempting brocantes (antiques
shops), with a glorious view. Take
the RF225 through the peaceful
Forêt de Bellême (see p62) as
far as the D931. Turn right for
Bellême (see p114). Go through
the town and turn right onto the
D203 to Nocé, where the **Auberge
des Trois J** (1 Pl Docteur-Gireaux)
is an excellent lunch stop.

AFTERNOON

Leave Nocé on the D9 and stop
off at the handsome turreted
Manoir de Courboyer, housing
the Maison du Parc du Perche.
You can visit the manor and
explore the extensive grounds,
which harbour orchards, ponds,
horses and donkeys. Regular
exhibitions and workshops are
held here. Head back onto the
D9, then turn right onto the
D5 to the impressive **Chapelle-
Montligeon**, a huge basilica built
in the early 1900s. After a look
around, and perhaps a detour to
the lovely **Forêt de Réno-Valdieu**
(see p62), head to the welcoming
Le Montligeon restaurant (14 Rue
Principale) for dinner.

See map on pp110–11 ←

Towns and Villages

1 Sées
MAP E5 ■ Tourist office: Pl du Général-de-Gaulle; 02 33 28 74 79

A bishopric since the 4th century, Sées has a few religious buildings: a Gothic cathedral with a very fine interior, a former Bishop's Palace and an abbey.

2 L'Aigle
MAP F5 ■ Tourist office: Pl Fulbert de Beina; 02 33 24 12 40

Traditionally a metalworking area, the town plays host each Tuesday to Normandy's biggest market *(see p77)*. St Martin's church and the château are both worth a visit.

3 Camembert
MAP E4 ■ Tourist Office: Rue de la Renaissance

Popularized by Napoleon III, the famous cheese was first made here by Marie Harel around 1790. Some farms still use her original method.

4 Argentan
MAP E5 ■ Tourist office: Pl du Marché; 02 33 67 12 48; www.tourisme-argentan-intercom.fr

Apart from its role at the end of the Battle of Normandy, commemorated by the nearby memorial, the town is known for lace and for horse racing.

5 St-Céneri-le-Gérei
MAP E6

Officially listed as one of France's top 100 prettiest, this small stone village above the River Sarthe has inspired generations of artists *(see p57)*.

6 Mortagne-au-Perche
MAP F6 ■ Tourist office: Pl de Gaulle; 02 33 83 34 37

Sometime regional capital, and an excellent base for exploring, this bustling, historic hilltop town is famous for its black pudding.

7 Bellême
MAP F6 ■ Tourist office: Blvd Bansard des Bois; 02 33 73 09 69

On a rocky spur overlooking forest, ruined fortifications nestle among well-preserved 17th- and 18th-century houses. There's a mushroom fair in late September.

8 Domfront
MAP D5 ■ Tourist office: Pl de la Roirie; www.ot-domfront.com

Perched above the Varenne Gorge, Domfront affords open views over the pear orchards of the Bocage Passais. The ramparts and castle are evidence of the town's turbulent history.

9 Mortain
MAP C5 ■ Tourist office: Rue du Bourg Lopin; 02 33 59 19 74

Mortain is surrounded by woods, granite and waterfalls. The Grande and Petite cascades are within easy walking distance of the town centre.

10 Pontorson
MAP B5 ■ Tourist office: Pl de l'Hôtel de Ville; 02 33 60 20 65

Pontorson is something of a gateway to Mont-St-Michel. Its 12th-century church is a fine example of Norman Romanesque architecture.

St-Céneri-le-Gérei

Museums and Attractions

Interior of the Église St-Julien

1 Église St-Julien, Domfront

MAP D5 ■ Pl du Commerce
■ Open 9am–7pm daily

Built of concrete in 1926, this church has Neo-Byzantine-style mosaics.

2 Ecomusée du Moulin de la Sée, Brouains

MAP C5 ■ 2 Le Moulin de Brouains ■ 02 33 49 76 64 ■ Open Apr & May: Sun; Jun & Sep: Wed–Sun; Jul & Aug: Tue–Sun ■ Adm

Admire the giant waterwheel that drove the machinery of this former paper mill on the River Sée.

3 Jardins de Pontgirard

MAP G6 ■ Monceaux-au-Perche ■ 02 33 73 61 49 ■ Open mid-Jun–Sep: 10am–6pm daily

Manoir du Pontgirard's glorious gardens feature lavender, an ancient lime tree and 30 kinds of euphorbia.

4 Fromagerie Durand

MAP E5 ■ Ferme de la Hérronière ■ 02 33 39 08 08 ■ Open 9am–5pm Tue–Sat ■ Adm

Visit one of the last fromageries to make Camembert in the traditional way, using unpasteurized milk.

5 La Maison du Camembert, Camembert

MAP F4 ■ Le Bourg ■ 02 33 12 10 37 ■ Open May–Sep: daily; Apr & Oct: Wed–Sun ■ Adm

Dedicated to the famous cheese, this museum features a reconstruction of an old production plant.

6 La Ferme du Cheval de Trait, Juvigny-sous-Andaine

MAP D5 ■ La Michaudière ■ Opening times vary, check website ■ Adm ■ www.lamichaudiere.fr

See horse-drawn agricultural equipment, a miniature farm and displays by Percheron draughthorses.

7 Musée de l'Emmigration Française au Canada, Tourouvre

MAP F5 ■ 15 Rue du Québec ■ Open Apr–Dec (times vary, check website) ■ Adm ■ www.musealesdetourouvre.fr

A replica of the room where, in the 17th-century, locals signed emigration contracts for Quebec.

8 Musée de la Dame aux Camélias, Gacé

MAP F5 ■ Château de Gacé ■ 02 33 67 08 59 ■ Open mid-Jun–mid-Sep (times vary, call ahead) ■ Adm

This museum evokes the extravagant lifestyle of the heroine of Alexandre Dumas' famous novel, set in the Orne.

Musée de la Dame aux Camélias

9 Musée et Prison Royale, Tinchebray

MAP D5 ■ 32 Grande Rue ■ 02 33 96 19 49 ■ Open Jul & Aug: 2:30–6pm Mon, Tue, Thu, Fri ■ Adm

A chilling place, with a court room, cells and an ethnographic museum.

10 Bellême Attelages

MAP F6 ■ La Maladrerie, Saint Martin du Vieux Bellême ■ 02 33 83 23 17 ■ Open mid-Mar–mid-Dec

Travel the Percheron countryside in a traditional horse-drawn carriage.

See map on pp110–11

Cultural Events

1 Les Féeriques, Falaise

MAP E4 ▪ www.falaise.fr ▪ early Dec–early Jan

The birthplace of William the Conqueror celebrates Christmas with lights, a craft market, fireworks and medieval-themed events.

2 Festival d'Accordéon, La Perche

02 33 89 58 03 ▪ Feb

Both up-and-coming musicians and renowned masters of the accordion appear on the playlist at this one-day festival.

3 Les Jeudis du Pin, Le Pin-au-Haras

Jun–mid-Sep: 3–4pm Thu

During the summer months, enjoy the weekly musical presentation of stallions, mares, foals and Norman donkeys at the prestigious national stud farm (see p112).

4 Les Musicales de Mortagne

MAP F6 ▪ Mortagne tourist office: 02 33 85 11 18 ▪ Late Jun–mid-Jul

In this celebration of music, six chamber concerts by world-class performers are staged in stunning settings in Mortagne-au-Perche.

5 Les Folklores du Monde, Alençon

MAP E6 ▪ www.lesfolkloresdumonde. com ▪ Jul

Alençon hosts this international folklore festival each year. The celebrations include concerts, processions and workshops.

6 Autour d'un Piano, Château de Carrouges

MAP E6 ▪ Office Départemental de la Culture: 02 33 31 25 42 ▪ www. ornetourisme.com ▪ Late Jul–Aug

This fine château makes for an even finer venue for recitals performed by famous soloists and chamber ensembles.

Les Musilumieres de Sées

7 Les Musilumières de Sées

MAP E5 ▪ www.musilumieres.org ▪ Jul–mid-Sep: Fri–Sat

The latest technology is used in this sound-and-light show at Sées's 13th-century Gothic cathedral (see p114).

8 Les Médiévales de Domfront

MAP D5 ▪ Maison des Associations: 02 33 38 56 66 ▪ www.domfront-medievales.com ▪ Aug

Every two years, actors and musicians re-create a medieval festival, with games and a market.

9 Festival des Voiles de Travail, Granville

MAP B5 ▪ www.festivaldesvoilesde travail.fr ▪ Late Aug

This five-day maritime-themed festival includes boat trips, concerts as well as local crafts.

10 Septembre Musical de l'Orne

02 33 26 99 99 ▪ www.septembre-musical.com ▪ Sep: Fri–Sun

Churches, abbeys and châteaux provide settings for opera, chamber music, jazz and dance events.

Places to Eat

PRICE CATEGORIES

For a three-course meal for one with half a bottle of wine (or equivalent meal), taxes and extra charges.

€ under €40   €€ €40–€60   €€€ over €60

1 La Grange de Tom, Champeaux

MAP B5 ▪ 40 Rte des Falaises ▪ 02 33 61 85 52 ▪ Closed Tue & Wed ▪ €

Set on the cliffs at Champeaux, this lovely former farm offers an irresistible view across the bay to Mont-St-Michel. The food, much of it grilled over an open fire, is a mix of traditional and modern.

2 Le Gué du Holme, St-Quentin-sur-le-Homme

MAP B5 ▪ 14 Rue des Estuaires ▪ 02 33 60 63 76 ▪ Closed Mon, Sat L, Sun D ▪ €

A range of fresh fish, local farm produce and game are among the choices at this restaurant (see p130).

3 Auberge du Terroir, Servon

MAP B5 ▪ Le Bourg ▪ 02 33 60 17 92 ▪ Closed Wed, Sat L ▪ €

Located in a small village close to Mont-St-Michel, this friendly, good-value restaurant with rooms serves dishes made from local ingredients.

4 Lion Verd, Putanges-Pont-Ecrepin

MAP E5 ▪ 02 33 35 01 86 ▪ €

This local favourite has a pretty riverside terrace by a bridge over the Orne. Vegetarian dishes are always on the menu.

5 Au Petit Vatel, Alençon

MAP E6 ▪ 72-74 Place du Commandant Desmeulle ▪ 02 33 28 47 67 ▪ Closed Tue, Wed & Sun D ▪ €€

This Alençon institution is well regarded for its sophisticated contemporary cuisine.

6 Chez François, Genêts

MAP B5 ▪ Prés de la Mairie ▪ 02 33 70 83 98 ▪ Closed Wed, Thu ▪ €

This cave-like bistro on the Bay of Mont-St-Michel is known for its grilled meats and delicious desserts. Vegetarian options are very limited.

7 Brit Hôtel du Dauphin, L'Aigle

MAP F5 ▪ Pl de la Halle ▪ 02 33 84 18 00 ▪ Restaurant closed Sun D (brasserie open daily) ▪ €€

The food at this comfortable, family-run hotel is excellent. Visitors can choose between the restaurant and brasserie.

8 Tribunal, Mortagne-au-Perche

MAP F6 ▪ 4 Pl du Palais ▪ 02 33 25 04 77 ▪ €

A choice of classic and regional dishes are offered at this old inn (see p128).

Tribunal, Mortagne-au-Perche

9 D'Une Ile, Rémalard-en-Perche

MAP G6 ▪ Lieu dit l'Aunay ▪ www.duneile.com ▪ €€

The kitchen at this country house serves seasonal cuisine. Advance booking is necessary.

10 Manoir du Lys, Bagnoles-de-l'Orne

MAP D5 ▪ La Croix Gauthier ▪ 02 33 37 80 69 ▪ www.manoir-du-lys.com ▪ €€€

Franck Quinton's cooking is rooted in local tradition but also respects contemporary trends.

See map on pp110–11

Streetsmart

Brightly coloured Camembert labels

Getting Around

Arriving by Air

With few international flights to Normandy, most air travellers fly to Paris and then take a train. **Ryanair** flies from Dublin and Manchester to Paris Beauvais; from the UK, **easyJet, Air France** and **British Airways** fly to Paris Charles de Gaulle. The region does have four small airports that cater to domestic flights. These can be found in **Caen-Carpiquet, Cherbourg, Le Havre** and **Rouen**. The French regional airline, **Air France Hop**, flies from Lyon to Caen.

International Train Travel

You can travel to France from the UK by taking your car on the **Eurotunnel** shuttle from Folkestone to Calais. The A16 motorway links Calais to Normandy, and the drive to Rouen takes 2 hours.

You can also travel from London St Pancras International to Paris Gare du Nord station by **Eurostar** trains, which take 2 hours 20 minutes. Travellers heading for Normandy can change at Lille for connections to towns such as Rouen and Bayeux. Tickets can be bought directly from the Eurostar website.

Regional and Local Trains

The state-owned national rail network, **SNCF**, links the region's major towns and cities. Fares are quite reasonable. For the ultra-fast TGVs (*Trains à Grande Vitesse*) you'll need to pay a supplement at peak times. All TGVs require numbered seat bookings. The slowest trains, marked TER on the timetables, stop at all stations. You do not need to make a reservation for regional TER trains; you do, however, need to for longer Intercity and night trains.

Tickets can be bought online at SNCF or **Rail Europe** and printed out or stored as QR codes on mobile phones. Tickets can also be purchased from machines at stations, they must then be inserted into yellow validating machines (located on every platform) before boarding. Failure to do so is deemed an offence.

Long-Distance Bus Travel

Deregulation in 2015 invigorated the previously almost non-existent long-haul coach business in France. **BlaBlaCar** runs a low-cost bus network which travels as far as London and Amsterdam, and includes several major French cities. BlaBlaCar also runs a service between Rennes and Caen.

Buses

Bus routes link many of the region's major destinations, although schedules are geared to students and commuters rather than tourists, so there's a reduced service at weekends. Coastal routes tend to be the most reliable. Different companies run the network for each *département*; tourist offices have the details. Costs can be reduced by buying tickets online rather than from the driver or board the bus. Get on the bus in the front and exit at the back or middle. Tickets for buses must be stamped in the validating machine.

Boats and Ferries

There are regular sailings from several UK ports across to Normandy.

Brittany Ferries sails to Cherbourg from both Portsmouth and Poole. Portsmouth to Cherbourg takes 3 hours, while Poole–Cherbourg is 4 hours 15 minutes. There are also crossings from Portsmouth to Le Havre (5 hours, 30 minutes day crossing and 10 hours night crossing), from Plymouth to Roscoff (6–8 hours) and also a Portsmouth–Caen route (6–8 hours). You can step off the ferry in the fishing port of Ouistreham, a short drive from Caen.

DFDS Seaways has two sailings per day to Dieppe from Newhaven, which take about 4 hours.

Motorists are advised to book ahead, especially in high season. Foot passengers and cyclists can normally just turn up and board. Prices vary enormously depending on the season and how far in advance you book. You can compare prices and find cut-price fares using the **Ferry Savers** website. Travellers can also reach Normandy by river from Paris. Two companies organize a romantic seven-night Seine cruise from Paris to Rouen, which stops at Vernon, Conflan and Les Andelys: **Viking River Cruises** and **CroisiEurope**. Their itineraries differ, but one of the CroisiEurope routes includes stops at Giverny, Rouen and Honfleur.

Public Transport

While the most rewarding way to take in any French town or city is on foot, public transport is highly developed, integrated and affordable. Buses are more affordable in France than in most of Europe. In Normandy there are bus services in all towns and cities, although they may not be air-conditioned and can be overcrowded.

Two cities in Normandy also operate tram systems which are efficient and affordable.

Trams

Both Rouen and Caen have modern tram systems. Rouen's is known locally as Métro de Rouen and operates from 4:30am (6:00am on Sunday) to 11:30pm. There is an underground branch which travels around the city centre and two overground routes which connect the southern suburbs. Caen's tram system connects the suburb regions with the city centre. Trams are operated by **Twisto** and run between 5:45am and 12:30am.

Guided Tours

A wide range of tours are available in Normandy, from boat rides around the coast and leisurely cycle rides to insightful D-Day tours.

Many companies offer D-Day tours around the northern beaches, mainly taking place in the summer months, such as the **Caen Memorial**, **Normandy Sightseeing Tours** and **D-Day Landing Tours**, the last two are based in Bayeux.

Boat trips are available from many of the sea ports. One of the best is the two-hour trip from Fécamp to Étretat, which allows you to get up close to the stunning cliff formations along the Côte d'Albâtre; contact the Fécamp tourist office for details. Guided river trips on the Douve and the Taute, near Carentan, which focus on the history, geography and environment of the marshlands, are also fun and informative.

DIRECTORY

Taxis

Official taxis are clearly identified. Taxis can only be picked up from taxi ranks (stations de taxi) or summoned by phone – not hailed on the street. Check your taxi has a meter before entering. Fares can vary from one *département* to another.

A number of apps have sprung up for summoning taxis, primarily in the cities, which can also be ordered by phones at taxi ranks. Billing begins from the moment of booking. **Uber** is popular throughout France, but beware of occasional rogue drivers in private vehicles.

Driving to Normandy

Bringing your own car to Normandy allows you to venture off track and travel at your own pace. For those driving from Britain to France, the simplest way is to use the Eurotunnel shuttles between Folkestone and Calais, both of which have direct motorway access. Normandy is also easily reachable from other European countries via E-roads, the International European Road Network connecting major roads across national borders within Europe.

To take your own foreign-registered car into and around France, you will need to carry the vehicle's registration and insurance documents, a full and valid driving licence, and valid passport or national ID at all times. EU driving licences are valid. An international driving licence (International Driving Permit or IDP) may be required for visitors from some countries outside the EU.

Car Rental

The major rental companies – for example **Europcar** and **Hertz** – operate in Normandy from airports, railway stations and city centres. To rent a car you must be 21 or over and have held a valid driver's licence for at least a year. You will also need a credit card for the rental deposit.

Rental cars with automatic transmission are rare, and must be booked in advance. Hire cars generally cannot be taken on ferries. Returning a car to a different location will incur surcharges. Before booking, look into fly-drive packages, which can be excellent value.

Driving in Normandy

The French love driving, and fast and spacious autoroutes (motorways) fan out throughout Normandy. With the exception of central Rouen's tricky one-way system, most cities in the region are car-friendly, with plenty of pay-and-display parking and car parks. Note that cities can be quite busy to drive through and parking is often more expensive than in the outskirts.

Parking regulations vary from place to place. Parking bays for which you have to pay are usually indicated with a blue Payant sign. Parking is normally limited to two hours. Drivers with disabilities holding a blue badge can park in marked spaces. However, parking on roads is not automatically free. In some time-restricted car parks, no time limit applies to blue-badge holders.

Road markings can be confusing. Depending on the type of road, four speed limits apply: on autoroutes, the limit is 130 kph (81 mph); on N or RN roads – dual carriageways – it's 110 kph (68 mph); on local D and minor C and V roads, it's 90 kph (56 mph); lastly, there's a limit of 50 kph (31 mph) in built-up areas.

Motorways in France have good rest areas (aires) every 10–20 km (6–12 miles). Petrol stations are located every 40 km (25 miles), these usually have restaurants, shops and other facilities.

The **RAC** has useful information on its website regarding driving in France.

Rules of the Road

Always drive on the right. Unless otherwise signposted, vehicles coming from the right have right of way. Cars on a roundabout usually have right of way. Seatbelts are compulsory, and it is prohibited to sound your horn in cities. Helmets and protective gloves are mandatory for motorcyclists and scooter riders throughout France.

By French law, you must carry ID, a driving licence, and car ownership and insurance details (you should take out emergency breakdown cover). You must add headlight beam deflectors to a right-hand drive car, and you should carry a red warning triangle, fire extinguisher, first-aid kit and a yellow reflective jacket.

If your car breaks down, wear your yellow reflective jacket and – walking behind the barrier for safety – place the red warning triangle 50–100 m (160–300 ft) behind it. If you have an accident, call the emergency services immediately. *Postes d'appel d'urgence* (emergency telephones) are posted at 2-km (1.5-mile) intervals on autoroutes, 4 km (2.5 miles) on dual carriageways; they will connect you with French rescue services via the traffic police.

In the city centres, it is against the law to use the bus lanes at any time of day. Using a mobile phone while driving can result in an immediate loss of licence. France strictly enforces a blood alcohol content limit of 0.05 per cent. By law, drivers must always carry a breathalyser device (€1 at petrol stations). French police can demand on-the-spot payment of traffic fines up to €750, and drug tests can be applied even for minor infractions.

Hitchhiking

Hitchhiking is forbidden on autoroutes and though it is legal on other roads, it is generally not recommended anywhere in France. Ride sharing with BlaBlaCar *(see p120)* is a safer, more popular alternative to hitchhiking. Fees are usually about a third of bus fares.

Cycle Hire

Cycling is very popular in Normandy and facilities are constantly improving. With its varied terrain, plentiful backroads and over 310 miles (500km) of cycling routes, the area is a wonderful region for cycling. You can transport your bike by air, rail (bicycles can be taken on nearly all SNCF trains) or ferry, or hire one in most towns and at some railway stations.

Rental prices are very reasonable in Normandy. **Ouibike** offer rentals throughout the region, while **Cy'clic** offer rentals in Rouen. **Freewheeling France** also have a useful website showing bike hire shops throughout other areas of the region. If you're after a mountain bike, look out for the VTT sign *(vélos tout terrain)*.

There are cycle paths throughout the region; tourist offices and local cycling associations can provide details. If you're feeling adventurous, you could cycle all the way from Paris to Mont-St-Michel on the **Veloscenic**, a stunning, long-distance cycle path that takes in some of Normandy's loveliest countryside – or opt to cycle just a section of it.

By law all children under 12 must wear helmets while cycling, even if just passengers.

Walking

Normandy is crisscrossed by hundreds of footpaths graded to suit walkers of all levels. The well-known *grande randonnée* (GR) trails, marked by red and white stripes, take walkers through some spectacular scenery. Regional tourist offices provide details and maps of all the GR routes in their *département*. The **French Federation of Hiking** also provides more information on GR routes on their website.

Walking in Normandy's cities and towns is also a great way to explore. Tourist offices in larger towns publish the useful "Circuit du Patrimoine", a city tour that takes in all the sights.

DIRECTORY

TAXIS

Uber
w uber.com

CAR RENTAL

Europcar
w europcar.com

Hertz
w hertz.com

DRIVING IN NORMANDY

RAC
w rac.co.uk

CYCLE HIRE

Cy'clic
w cyclic.rouen.fr

Freewheeling France
w freewheelingfrance. com

Ouibike
w ouibike.net

Veloscenic
w velocscenic.com

WALKING

French Federation of Hiking
w ffrandonnee.fr

Practical Information

Passports and Visas

For entry requirements, including visas, consult your nearest French embassy or check the French **Ministry of Foreign Affairs** website. No visa is required for citizens of EU countries, the UK, USA, Canada, Australia or New Zealand for stays of less than 3 months, although your passport will need to be valid for at least 3 months beyond the end of your stay. Citizens of other countries should consult their nearest French embassy or consulate for information before travelling.

Government Advice

Now more than ever, it is important to consult both your and the French government's advice before travelling. The **UK Foreign and Commonwealth Office**, the **US State Department**, the **Australian Department of Foreign Affairs and Trade** and **Gouvernement France** offer the latest advice on security, health and local regulations.

Customs Information

You can find information on the laws relating to goods and currency taken in or out of France on the official **France Tourism** website. For EU citizens there are no limits on goods that can be taken into or out of France if they are for your personal use. The laws differ for those outside the EU.

Insurance

We recommend that you take out a comprehensive policy covering theft, loss of belongings, medical care, cancellations and delays, and read the small print carefully. UK and EU citizens are eligible for discounted or free emergency medical care in France provided they have a valid EHIC (European Health Insurance Card) or **GHIC** (UK Global Health Insurance Card).

Health

France has a world-class healthcare system. All EU and UK nationals holding an EHIC or GHIC are entitled to use the French national health service. Patients must pay for treatment and can reclaim most of the cost from the health authorities. The process may be lengthy and travellers should consider purchasing private travel insurance. For visitors from outside the EU and the UK, payment of hospital and other medical expenses is the patient's responsibility. It is therefore important to arrange comprehensive medical insurance before traveling.

If you are staying in a hotel, staff should be able to recommend an English-speaking doctor, or put you in touch with the 24-hour *médecin de garde* (doctor service) that operates in every major town. You can also consult the local pharmacist or the telephone operator.

Pharmacies (chemists), indicated by a green cross, are usually very helpful for minor ailments or injuries. Opening hours are 9am–7pm Monday to Saturday, but one pharmacy in every town will be open at night and at weekends.

Local dentists are listed in local *Pages Jaunes* (Yellow Pages). In an emergency, you will be seen in the accident and emergency department of a major hospital.

Unless stated otherwise, tap water in France is safe to drink.

For information regarding COVID-19 vaccination requirements, consult government advice.

Smoking, Alcohol and Drugs

Smoking is prohibited in all public places, but is allowed on restaurant, café and pub outside terraces, as long as they are not enclosed.

The possession of narcotics is prohibited and could result in a prison sentence.

Unless stated otherwise, alcohol consumption on the streets is permitted.

ID

There is no requirement for visitors to carry ID, but in the event of a routine check you may be asked to show your passport. If you don't have it with you, the police may escort you to wherever your passport is being kept.

Personal Security

Normandy is a relatively safe place to travel and

most visits are trouble-free. Beware of pick pockets in major tourist areas and on city buses during rush hour. If anything is stolen, report it as soon as possible to the nearest police station, and bring ID with you. Get a copy of the crime report in order to claim on your insurance. Contact your embassy if you have your passport stolen, or in the event of a serious crime or accident.

If you lose your passport, report it to the police immediately. Next, inform your embassy or consulate –most are in Paris, though there are some consulates in Rouen, Le Havre and Caen. Make copies of all important documents and keep them separately.

For emergency **police, fire department** or **ambulance** services call 112 – the operator will ask which service you require. For medical emergencies you can also dial 15 for **SAMU (ambulance)**. The direct number for the **police** is 17 and for the **fire department** it is 18.

As a rule, residents of Normandy are very accepting of all people, regardless of their race, gender or sexuality. Same-sex marriage was legalized in 2013 and France recognized the right to legally change your gender in 2016.

Women may receive more attention, especially around tourist areas. Open staring and verbal flirtation is not uncommon. If you feel threatened, head straight for the nearest police station.

Travellers with Specific Requirements

A number of companies are working to improve accessibility across the region of Normandy.

Jaccede has details of accessible sights in Rouen and other cities. Rail operator SNCF (see p120) provides a booking service for free assistance on TGVs. **Les Compagnons du Voyage** provides assistants for people with limited mobility or visibility on any form of public transport, for a small fee.

Normandy Tourism's website as well as the organization **Coordination Handicap Normandie** list sights, hotels and restaurants that are accessible for visitors with limited mobility or visual or hearing impairment.

Tourism for All, in the UK, has a useful list of specialist tour operators, and **Sage Traveling** also offers a variety of packages and assistance.

For further information on accessibility, contact the French disability advocacy group **GIHP**.

DIRECTORY

PASSPORTS AND VISAS

Ministry of Foreign Affairs
w diplomatie.gouv.fr

GOVERNMENT ADVICE

Australian Department of Foreign Affairs and Trade
w smartraveller.gov.au

Gouvernement France
w gouvernement.fr

UK Foreign and Commonwealth Office
w gov.uk/foreign-travel-advice

US Department of State
w travel.state.gov

CUSTOMS INFORMATION

France Tourism
w ee.france.fr

INSURANCE

GHIC
w nhs.uk

PERSONAL SECURITY

Medical Help/Ambulance (SAMU)
C 15

Fire Brigade
C 18

Police
C 17

SOS – All Services
C 112

TRAVELLERS WITH SPECIFIC REQUIREMENTS

Coordination Handicap Normandie
w handicap-normandie.org

GIHP
w gihpnational.org

Jaccede
w jaccede.com

Les Compagnons du Voyage
w compagnons.com

Normandy Tourism
w en.normandie-tourisme.fr

Sage Traveling
w sagetraveling.com

Tourism for All
w tourismforall.org.uk

Time Zone

France is in the Central European Time Zone (GMT+1): 1 hour ahead of the UK, 6 hours ahead of Eastern Standard Time and 9 hours ahead of Pacific Standard Time.

Money

France is one of the many European countries using the euro (€). Most establishments in Normandy accept major credit, debit and prepaid currency cards, but it's always a good idea to carry some cash too (which may be expected for purchases under €15).

Some foreign cards – North American ones, in particular – may not be recognized by ATMs, unstaffed toll booths and petrol pumps. Smaller shops, hotels, restaurants and campsites generally prefer payment in cash.

Electrical Appliances

Electricity runs on 220V using double, round-pin sockets. You may need to bring an adapter, and possibly a transformer (especially for US electrical appliances).

Mobile phones and Wi-Fi

With 5G coverage now widespread, France offers strong mobile signals throughout. Free Wi-Fi hotspots are widely available in public spaces. Cafés and restaurants usually permit the use of their Wi-Fi to customers who make a purchase. Visitors with EU tariffs will be able to use their devices abroad without being affected by data roaming charges. Users will be charged the same rates for data, SMS and voice calls as they would pay at home. Those not on EU tariffs should check roaming rates with their provider. A cheaper option may be to purchase a French SIM card (you will need to show ID).

Postal Services

French post offices, easily identifiable by their yellow and blue "La Poste" sign, open 9am–noon and 2–5pm Monday to Friday, and Saturday mornings. You can buy stamps in *tabacs* (tobacconists), as well as post offices.

Weather

Normandy's climate is temperate. Summers can be pleasantly hot. Spring and autumn are mild, with a fair amount of rain, but there are also wonderfully bright days. Winter is cold, but this is one of the least crowded seasons to visit and the light at this time of year can make Mont-St-Michel look almost ethereal.

Opening Hours

Food shops tend to open from 9am to 7pm Monday to Saturday, with a lunch break from noon to 2pm. Non-food shops generally open between 9am and 6pm, from Monday to Saturday, and also close for lunch. Hypermarkets, supermarkets, department stores and shops in city centres and tourist towns usually stay open at lunch. On Sundays most shops are closed, though some *boulangeries* and *pâtisseries* open in the morning.

Museums are generally open from 10am to 5pm but are closed during lunch. Most museums are closed on either Monday or Tuesday. Banks are usually open from Monday to Friday, between 9am and 4pm, with some closing over lunch.

Banks, shops and restaurants are closed on New Year's Day, Easter Monday, 1 May (Labour Day), 8 May (VE Day), Ascension Day (40 days after Easter), Whitsun (7th Sun after Easter), Whit Monday, 14 July (Bastille Day), 15 August (Assumption), 1 November (All Saints' Day), 11 November (Armistice Day) and 25 December (Christmas Day).

COVID-19 Increased rates of infection may result in temporary opening hours and/or closures. Always check ahead before visiting museums, attractions and hospitality venues.

Visitor Information

Valuable sources of information include the **Normandy Tourism Board** (*Comité Régional du Tourisme*), based in Évreux, and each of Normandy's five *départements*, which have their own **tourist offices** (*Comité Départemental du Tourisme*). It's worth consulting their websites when you are planning your trip.

All cities and most towns also have a state-run tourist office. Some smaller towns and villages have a private *Syndicat d'Initiative* (SI).

The **Normandy War Guide** website has information for those wishing to visit the sites of the D-Day landings.

Local Customs

Etiquette *(la politesse)* is important to the French. On entering and leaving a store or café, you are expected to say *"bonjour"* and *"au revoir"* to staff. Be sure to add *"s'il vous plaît"* (please) when ordering, and *"pardon"* if you accidentally bump into someone. The French usually shake hands on meeting someone for the first time.

Friends and colleagues who know each other well greet each other with a kiss on each cheek. If you are unsure about what's expected, wait to see if they proffer a hand or a cheek.

Language

French is the official language, but English is increasingly understood, especially among the young. A few niceties will go a long way – try to say at least *"bonjour"* before switching to English.

Taxes and Refunds

VAT is around 20 per cent in France. Non-EU residents can claim back tax on certain goods and purchases over €175.

Look out for the Global Refund Tax-Free sign, and ask the retailer for a form for a détaxe receipt. Present the goods receipt, détaxe receipt and passport at customs when you depart to receive your refund.

Accommodation

France offers a huge variety of accommodation, comprising luxury five-star hotels, family-run B&Bs, budget hostels and private apartments.

Local tourist offices are helpful for accommodation on farms and gîtes which are good options if you prefer a less impersonal set-up. *Fermes auberges* (farm stays) are working farms with simple restaurants and a few bedrooms. B&Bs *(chambres d'hôtes)* are also a good option and often less expensive than hotels. Self-catering holiday homes and camping are ideal for families staying for a week or more.

Accommodation in *gîtes* is also plentiful. Often these are pretty cottages or farmhouses – most of them privately owned. Crockery and kitchen utensils are supplied, and bed linen and cleaning can usually be provided for a small extra charge.

If you plan on visiting Normandy in high season, it would be wise to book well ahead. Normandy is a popular destination from spring to autumn, but from early July to late August the resorts in particular are at their busiest. There are some smaller hotels in rural

areas that close from November to March.

Note that hotels offer substantial discounts for advance online bookings.

Places to Stay

PRICE CATEGORIES
For a standard double room per night (with breakfast if included), including taxes and extra charges.

€ under €100 €€ €100–€250 €€€ over €250

Luxury Hotels

Belle-Isle-sur-Risle
MAP F3 ▪ 112 Rte de Rouen, Pont Audemer ▪ 02 32 56 96 22 ▪ www.bellile.com ▪ €€
This idyllic 19th-century manor is set on its own little wooded island in the middle of the Risle. The 28 rooms are elegant and comfortable, while the excellent gourmet restaurant serves creative dishes using seasonal ingredients. Facilities include indoor and out-door swimming pools.

Grand Hôtel, Cabourg
MAP E3 ▪ Prom Marcel-Proust ▪ 02 31 91 01 79 ▪ www.all.accor.com ▪ €€
Celebrated for its association with Marcel Proust, who spent his childhood holidays here and famously described the dining room as an aquarium, this huge white edifice is still redolent of its *belle époque* heyday, with vast rooms. The façade of the hotel faces the town, while the rear opens out onto the beach.

Hôtel Bourgtheroulde, Rouen
MAP L5 ▪ 15 Pl de la Pucelle ▪ 02 35 14 50 50 ▪ www.hotelsparouen.com ▪ €€
This boutique hotel, set in a beautiful 16th-century building, has a chic atrium bar, plus a restaurant, spa and an illuminated swimming pool.

Le Manoir des Impressionistes, Honfleur
MAP F3 ▪ 23 Rte de Trouville ▪ 02 31 81 63 00 ▪ www.manoirdesimpressionnistes.com ▪ €€
Minutes away from the bustle of Honfleur, most of the rooms in this small manor overlook the Seine estuary. Each room has been styled individually, and residents have first call on the restaurant.

Château de la Chenevière, Port-en-Bessin
MAP C3 ▪ Escures-Commes ▪ 02 31 51 25 25 ▪ www.lacheneviere.com ▪ €€€
With 19 rooms and ten suites, this elegant 18th-century château, standing in its own parkland, has the feel of a great English country house. It makes an ideal base for visiting the D-Day beaches.

La Ferme St-Siméon, Honfleur
MAP F3 ▪ Rue A-Marais ▪ 02 31 81 78 00 ▪ www.fermesaintsimeon.fr ▪ €€€
This ancient farmhouse on the Seine estuary, once a meeting place for Impressionist painters, is now the most luxurious (and expensive) country hotel in Normandy.

Normandy Barrière, Deauville
MAP E3 ▪ 38 Rue Mermoz ▪ 02 31 98 66 22 ▪ www.hotelsbarriere.com ▪ €€€
With its rambling timber-framed façade, this hotel has the air of a quaint Norman cottage built for a giant. Inside, there are chandeliers and columns, an indoor swimming pool around which breakfast can be served, and a handy underground passage leading to Deauville Casino, which is owned by the same hotel and leisure group.

Hotels with Character

Tribunal, Mortagne-au-Perche
MAP F6 ▪ 4 Pl du Palais ▪ 02 33 25 04 77 ▪ www.hotel-tribunal.fr ▪ €
Occupying a handsome building with origins in the 13th century, this welcoming central hotel is an excellent base for exploring the Perche. It also has an excellent restaurant *(see p117)*.

Ferme de la Rançonnière, Crépon
MAP D3 ▪ Rte d'Arromanches ▪ 02 31 22 21 73 ▪ www.ranconniere.fr ▪ €€
Early inhabitants of this medieval fortified farm tried to keep people out; the present incumbents are far more welcoming. On Sundays, the two dining rooms only just manage to keep pace with the regulars. The rooms are comfortable and elegant.

Hostellerie de la Vieille Ferme

MAP H1 ▪ Criel-sur-Mer ▪ 02 35 86 72 18 ▪ www.vieille-ferme.net ▪ €€

Choose from smartly decorated rooms in the 18th-century main building, the Anglo-Norman style pavillion or one of the two villas dating back to the early 19th century. On-site spa and sauna are also available.

Hôtel d'Outre-Mer, Villers-sur-Mer

MAP E3 ▪ 1 Rue du Maréchal Leclerc ▪ 02 31 87 04 64 ▪ www.hotel outremer.com ▪ €€

At this novel boutique-style hotel near the beach, every room is decorated in a different colour scheme. The hotel also has a quirky library with board games, and the general feel is hip but laid back.

Le Grand Hard

MAP B3 ▪ Sainte-Marie-Du-Mont ▪ 02 33 71 25 74 ▪ www.legrandhard.fr ▪ €€

Only a 15-minute drive from Utah Beach (see p103) this converted farmhouse is built around a pretty courtyard. Ideal for families, it has five family rooms, plus an in-house restaurant and fitness room. Extras include bicycles and children's toys and games.

Le Moulin de Connelles, Connelles

MAP H3 ▪ Rte d'Amfreville- sous-les-Monts ▪ 02 32 59 53 33 ▪ www.moulin-de-connelles.fr ▪ €€

When you see the turreted mill's reflection between the lily pads that float beneath the restaurant window, you know you are in picture-postcard territory. A small, very comfortable hotel, with beautiful bathrooms and a superb restaurant.

Perché dans le Perche, Bellou-Le-Trichard

MAP H6 ▪ La Renardière ▪ 02 33 25 57 96 ▪ www.perchedansleperche.com ▪ €€

Arguably Normandy's most unusual place to stay, this is the treehouse of your childhood dreams, kitted out with comfy beds and modern facilities, set in a 200-year-old sweet chestnut tree. The terrace completely envelops the trunk, giving panoramic views of the countryside.

Seaside Hotels

L'Augeval, Deauville

MAP E3 ▪ 15 Ave Hocquart de Turtot ▪ 02 31 81 13 18 ▪ www.augeval.com ▪ €

In the heart of Deauville, a short distance from the casino and glitzy seafront boardwalk, the delightful L'Augeval comprises two listed Anglo-Norman-style villas. Rooms have spa baths and there is a large heated pool.

Dormy House, Étretat

MAP F2 ▪ Rte Le Havre ▪ 02 35 27 07 88 ▪ www.dormy-house.com ▪ €€

With an Art Deco-style main building and two (rather more comfortable) annexes, this hotel sits among greenery, with fine views over the town, the sea and Étretat's famous cliffs, Falaises d'Aval and d'Amont. The breakfasts are exceptional.

Hôtel de la Marine, Barneville-Carteret

MAP A3 ▪ 11 Rue de Paris ▪ 02 33 53 83 31 ▪ www.hotelmarine.com ▪ Closed mid-Dec–mid-Feb ▪ €€

La Marine is well known for its Michelin-starred restaurant (see p109), which has splendid views over the harbour. But being so close to all the superb beaches on the Cotentin Peninsula's west coast, it also makes an excellent base for a seaside holiday.

Hôtel des Ormes, Barneville-Carteret

MAP A3 ▪ Prom Barbey-d'Aurevilly ▪ 02 33 52 23 50 ▪ www.hotel-restaurant-les-ormes.fr ▪ €€

The ultimate seaside hotel in Normandy, this charming establishment sits right on the beach. It has a fine restaurant, a tranquil garden and lovely views over the marina.

La Terrasse, Varengeville-sur-Mer

MAP G1 ▪ Vasterival ▪ 02 35 85 12 54 ▪ www.hotel-restaurant-la-terrasse.com ▪ Closed mid-Nov–mid-Mar ▪ €€

A narrow lane winds through typical Norman countryside to the cliff's edge and this characterful small hotel with cosy rooms. There are magical sea views from the covered terrace, where meals are served in summer.

Le Flaubert, Trouville-sur-Mer

MAP E3 ▪ Rue Gustave Flaubert ▪ 02 31 88 37 23 ▪ www.flaubert.fr ▪ €€

Situated on the beach, the Flaubert is a glorious place to stay in Trouville, one of the birthplaces of Impressionism.

Le Landemer, Urville-Nacqueville

MAP A2 ▪ 2 Rue des Douanes ▪ 02 33 04 05 10 ▪ www.le-landemer.com ▪ €€

This beautifully renovated hotel is set at the end of a beach and has a fantastic restaurant. It offers ten spotless rooms, each with a panoramic sea view, and some with their own private terrace. The staff are extremely helpful.

Country Hotels

Le Gué du Holme, St-Quentin-sur-le-Homme

MAP B5 ▪ 14 Rue des Estuaires ▪ 02 33 60 63 76 ▪ www.le-gue-du-holme.com ▪ €

Michel Leroux, the chef at this hotel-restaurant, is probably the best for miles in any direction. Any thought of driving onward after your meal should be dispelled by the comfy rooms – most of them in a modern wing overlooking a rose garden.

Verte Campagne, Trelly

MAP B4 ▪ Le Hameau Chevalier ▪ 02 33 47 65 33 ▪ www.laverte campagne.com ▪ €

This ivy-covered 16th-century Norman farmhouse is located in the heart of the countryside and retains its charming beams and bare stone walls. The bedrooms are very comfortable and the atmospheric downstairs restaurant serves well-presented, thoughtful menus of seasonal local dishes.

Château de Boucéel, Vergoncey

MAP B5 ▪ Lieu-dit Boucéel ▪ 02 33 48 34 61 ▪ www. chateaudebouceel.com ▪ €€

This lovely 1760s château near the Bay of Mont-St-Michel is run by the descendants of its original owners. Its palatial rooms represent superb value; there are also cottages for rent in the grounds.

Château de la Rapée, Gisors

MAP J3 ▪ Bazincourt-sur-Epte ▪ 02 32 55 11 61 ▪ www.hotel-la-rapee. com ▪ €€

At the end of a rutted forest track, this Gothic mansion offers spacious rooms with fine furniture, lovely views and excellent food in the restaurant.

Country Lodge, Perche

MAP G6 ▪ Parc Naturel Régional du Perche ▪ www.country-lodge. com ▪ €€

An idyllic lodge set among wooded hills, this working farm offers accommodation in 24 wooden cabins, sleeping from four to 13 people.

D'Une Île, Rémalard

MAP G6 ▪ Domaine de Launay, Lieu dit L'Aunay ▪ 02 33 83 01 47 ▪ www. duneile.com ▪ €€

This picturesque collection of medieval cottages in the idyllic Perche countryside contains seven beautifully renovated rooms and two family apartments. Communal dinners, made using carefully sourced local produce, are served in the con-

verted stable block or in the delightful courtyard in warm weather.

La Réserve, Giverny

MAP H4 ▪ La Réserve Fond des Marettes ▪ 02 32 21 99 09 ▪ www.giverny-lareserve.com ▪ €€

More a luxury B&B than a hotel, La Réserve is arguably the best place to stay in the Giverny area. Its five rooms are full of light and tastefully decorated with beautiful antiques and floral soft furnishings. The service is charming and personal.

Le Castel, Montpinchon

MAP B4 ▪ 02 33 17 00 45 ▪ www.le-castel-normandy.com ▪ €€

In July and August, this sumptuous château in rural surroundings specializes in all-inclusive packages for families, with accommodation in two-bedroom suites, plenty of outdoor activities for children and relaxing evening meals for the parents. In April, May, September and October, it operates as a regular B&B and makes a great country retreat.

Chambres d'Hôte (B&B)

Le Colombier

MAP G1 ▪ Mr et Mme Duval, Bertrimont ▪ 02 32 80 14 24 ▪ www.le-colombier.net ▪ €

An 18th-century round *colombier* (dovecote) has been lovingly restored to provide characterful accommodation at this traditional Norman farm. Two additional rooms are available in the main farmhouse. Guests can enjoy homemade cider and delicious breakfasts at this quaint B&B.

Le Domaine de Pasiphae, Vimoutiers

MAP F4 ▪ 13 Ave Foch ▪ 02 33 35 97 65 ▪ www. domainedepasiphae.com ▪ €

Located around 10 minutes' walk from the centre of Vimoutiers and ideal for exploring the Pays d'Auge, this handsome, red-brick town house set in immaculate grounds offers three charming, rooms, one with a balcony overlooking the garden, another with its own cosy little salon. The breakfast is excellent and you can also have evening meals (barbecues in summer) with 48 hours' advance notice.

Le Manoir des Etilleux, Les Etilleux

MAP F6 ▪ Lieu-dit Le Boulay ▪ 06 03 57 33 56 ▪ www.manoirdes etilleux.fr ▪ €

Set in the lovely Perche countryside, this graceful old manor house has four spacious rooms and a gîte, all comfortably and elegantly furnished. There is a wellness area and tennis court for guests. The breakfasts include homemade jams and bread.

Le Manoir des Lions de Tourgéville, Deauville

MAP E3 ▪ Le Bourg ▪ 02 31 88 84 95 ▪ www. manoirlionstourgeville. com ▪ €

This is a very elegant and welcoming *manoir*, with a lovely garden, just outside Deauville. The spacious rooms are

decorated with lots of beautiful antiques, and equipped with modern bathrooms. Breakfasts here are sumptuous.

Maison du Docteur Vassaux, Saint-Saëns

MAP H2 ▪ 148 Rue du Docteur Vassaux ▪ 02 35 61 67 28 ▪ www. saintsaens-chambres-dhote.com ▪ €

Henri Matisse was a frequent visitor to the Vassaux family, who once occupied this characterful, timber-framed town house in the centre of the village of Saint-Saëns, a handy overnight stop on the way to or from the port of Dieppe. The rooms are tastefully decorated and there's a lovely garden at the rear.

Château de Sarceaux, Alençon

MAP E6 ▪ Rue des Fourneaux ▪ 02 33 28 85 11 ▪ www.chateau-de-sarceaux.com ▪ €€

Guests at this charming château, a former hunting lodge, are welcomed by the Marquis and Marquise, no less. Accommodation comprises four elegant, antique-furnished rooms, overlooking the beautiful grounds and lake, while a converted stable block can accommodate a larger group or family.

La Cour Ste-Catherine, Honfleur

MAP F3 ▪ 74 Rue du Puits ▪ 07 87 04 49 16 ▪ www. coursaintecatherine.com ▪ €€

This charming B&B, close to the old port, is housed in a 17th-century building that used to be a convent. The five rooms (one per floor) feature

en-suite bathrooms. Nearby are three self-catering apartments that sleep five.

Manoir de la Fieffe

MAP B2 ▪ Cherbourg-en-Cotentin ▪ 02 33 20 81 45 ▪ www.manoir delafieffe.com ▪ €€

A 16th-century manor house, the Manoir de la Fieffe has a rich history. It offers three clean and spacious bedrooms as well as a self-catering cottage. Guests can relax in the enormous park that surrounds the manor.

Tanquerey de la Rochaisière, Coutances

MAP B4 ▪ 13 Rue St-Martin ▪ 06 50 57 22 55 ▪ www.bandb-hotel-coutances.fr ▪ €€

Right in the centre of Coutances, but located on a quiet street, this very welcoming B&B, in a 17-century townhouse, offers two huge and sumptuously furnished rooms. In warm weather guests can sit outside in the courtyard garden.

Budget Hotels

La Ferme des Mares, Saint-Germain-Sur-Ay

MAP B3 ▪ 26 Rue des Mares ▪ 02 33 17 01 02 ▪ www.la-ferme-des-mares.com ▪ €

Located in a tranquil spot on the west coast of the Cotentin peninsula, this traditional family-owned farmhouse has ten spacious rooms. The delicious home-cooked meals lend to its homely, welcoming charm.

For a key to hotel price categories see p128

La Régence, Cherbourg

MAP B2 ■ 42 Quai de Caligny ■ 02 33 43 05 16 ■ www.laregence.com ■ €
Facing the quay, this popular bistro offers small, tastefully dec- orated rooms, some with spa baths. Opt for a room overlooking the port. It makes a decent base in a town that is not noted for its hotels.

Le Cap, Barneville-Carteret

MAP A3 ■ 6 Rue du Port ■ 02 33 53 85 89 ■ www. hotel-le-cap.fr ■ €
A welcoming seafront hotel, with basic but appealing rooms, some with sea views. The restaurant has a strong local following for its excellent seafood and traditional cuisine.

Les Agriculteurs, St-Pierre-sur-Dives

MAP E4 ■ 118 Rue de Falaise ■ 02 31 20 72 78 ■ www.lesagriculteurs. com ■ €
This long-established, family-run Logis de France has a cosy atmosphere, pretty bedrooms, and a popular local restaurant serving regional food. Time your visit for the Monday market (see p76).

Logis Les Ramparts, Bayeux

MAP C3 ■ 4 Rue Bourbesneur ■ 02 31 92 50 40 ■ www.lecornu.fr ■ €
Owned by François Lecornu, the only cider producer within Bayeux town, this charming hotel has bags of char- acter. The rooms are

all non-smoking and beautifully decorated with antiques, but have no TVs. The hotel is not accessible to guests with disabilities.

Moulin Fouret, Bernay

MAP F4 ■ St Aubin le Vertueux ■ 07 81 68 42 07 ■ www.moulin-fouret. fr ■ €
This handsome 16th- century watermill is primarily known for its high-quality restaurant, but it also has some simple, good-value en-suite rooms, some with views of the garden or river. You can dine outside in summer in the flower-filled garden.

Aux 13 Arches, Portbail

MAP A3 ■ 9 Pl Castel ■ 02 33 04 87 90 ■ www. 13arches.com ■ €€
This cool little hotel- restaurant is situated right by the seashore in a tiny harbour near Barneville-Carteret. Rooms are simple and elegant and overlook a decked area.

Self-Catering Holidays

Allez France

www.allezfrance.com
The properties offered by this long-established UK company range from modern apartments to stone or timbered cottages, most of which are French-owned.

Brittany Ferries

0330 159 7000 ■ www. brittany-ferries.co.uk
Brittany Ferries offer good value ferry-plus- accomodation deals in the north of France.

Self-catering property options range from small gîtes to large detached villas with a pool.

Cottages.com

www.cottages.com
This company lists cottages – more than 120 of them – near a variety of attractions: among others, the D-Day landing sites, golf courses, Mont-St- Michel and beaches. The website includes previous visitors' com- ments and cottages categorized according to amenities available. They will also make travel arrangements for you.

French Connections

www.frenchconnections. co.uk
French Connections offers a large range of accommodation, from luxury converted barns to quaint country cottages. The majority of their houses in Normandy are owned by private individuals. The website carries full descriptions and lots of photographs of each property and, where possible, provides links to the owner's own website.

Gîtes de France

08 00 60 08 10 ■ www. gites-de-france- normandie.com
The Fédération Nationale des Gîtes de France has more than 2,000 classified properties in Normandy, mostly quaint rural cot- tages, and should be the first stop for anyone planning a self-catering holiday in the region.

Novasol
www.novasol.co.uk
This large web portal lists rentals in 26 countries, including nearly 3,000 quality properties in France, ranging from small stone cottages to half-timbered houses, or fully modernized apartments with swimming pools.

Campsites

Camping de la Vée, Bagnoles-de-l'Orne
MAP D5 ▪ 5 Rue du Président Coty ▪ 02 33 37 87 45 ▪ www.campingbagnolesdelorne.com ▪ Closed end Nov–Feb ▪ €
The joy of La Vée is its position – close to Bagnoles (see p66) and the Fôret des Andaines (see p63). Its 250 pitches are set in leafy surrounds, and its many amenities include a snack bar and games room.

Camping de l'Ermitage, Donville-les-Bains
MAP B4 ▪ 02 33 50 09 01 ▪ www.camping-ermitage.com ▪ Closed mid-Oct–mid-Apr ▪ €
With its own delicatessen, snack bar and visiting traders, you seldom need to leave this large, well-run campsite. As well as the beach, you can ride, play tennis, or relax in the thalassotherapy centre.

Camping des Deux Rivières, Martigny
MAP H1 ▪ 02 35 85 60 82 ▪ www.camping-2-rivieres.com ▪ Closed mid-Oct–late Mar ▪ €
It's hard to believe, but this peaceful campsite tucked away on an island is only a short drive from Dieppe. There are plenty of indoor amusements, but with the Arques Forest, Varenne River and a lake on the doorstep, this is really a place for outdoor types.

Camping du Vievre, St-Georges-du-Vièvre
MAP F3 ▪ 02 32 42 76 79 ▪ www.camping-eure-normandie.fr ▪ Closed Oct–Mar ▪ €
Most of the campers here are fresh-air fiends, drawn by the prospect of energetic hikes through the countryside or taxing mountain bike rides. If that sounds too much like hard work, there is also tennis, table tennis and a pool on site.

Camping Huttopia, Moyaux
MAP F3 ▪ 04 37 64 22 35 ▪ www.europe.huttopia.com ▪ Closed mid-Sep–Apr ▪ €
A traditional, upmarket campsite – with no caravans – in the grounds of an elegant château, where (if you book) you can dine on Tuesday and Saturday. It has a heated pool, bar, crêperie, grocery, games room and mini golf.

La Côte de Nacre, St-Aubin-sur-Mer
MAP G1 ▪ Rue Général Moulton ▪ 04 11 32 90 00 ▪ www.sandaya.fr ▪ Closed Oct–Apr ▪ €
With a superb swimming pool, water chutes, kids' activities and organized entertainment, this is a great family-oriented five-star campsite.

La Vallée, Houlgate
MAP E3 ▪ 88 Rte de la Vallée ▪ 02 31 24 40 69 ▪ www.campinglavallee.co.uk ▪ Closed Oct–Mar ▪ €
This very large and well-equipped site is just a short walk from Houlgate beach, where you can take sailing lessons and go sea fishing.

Le Ranch, Le Rozel
MAP A2 ▪ 02 33 10 07 10 ▪ www.camping-leranch.com ▪ Closed Oct–Apr ▪ €
Pitch a tent, or stay in one of the site's well-designed caravans. Situated on the west coast of the Cotentin, Le Ranch has access to a vast, fine sandy beach, a good place for serious surfing.

Les Gravelets, Montmartin-sur-Mer
MAP B4 ▪ 3 Rue du Rey ▪ 02 33 47 70 20 ▪ www.camping-montmartin.com ▪ Closed Nov–Mar ▪ €
This two-star seaside campsite was converted from a lime quarry in 1983. One of the pits is now used for rock climbing; the other has been turned into tennis courts. You can catch your own seafood and cook it over a campfire.

Château de Lez Eaux, St-Pair-sur-Mer
MAP B5 ▪ 02 33 51 66 09 ▪ www.lez-eaux.com ▪ Closed end Sep–end Mar ▪ €€
Large, luxury "pitches", and wood cabins are offered at this four-star campsite. If you tire of the aquapark, tennis, volleyball and billiards, Mont-St-Michel, Granville and Brittany are all within easy reach.

For a key to hotel price categories see p128

General Index

Acknowledgments

Authors

Fiona Duncan and Leonie Glass are a British travel-writing team of long standing. They are co-authors of *DK Eyewitness Travel Guide Top 10 Amsterdam*, as well as numerous guides for Duncan Petersen, including *Paris Walks* in the *On the Foot Guide* series and several of the *Charming Small Hotel* Guides. Fiona Duncan is a frequent contributor to the *Daily Telegraph*'s Travel pages.

Additional Contributor Ruth Reisenberger

Publishing Director Georgina Dee

Publisher Vivien Antwi

Design Director Phil Ormerod

Editorial Kate Berens, Michelle Crane, Rachel Fox, Scarlett O'Hara, Sally Schafer, Sophie Wright

Cover Design Bess Daly, Maxine Pedliham

Design Tessa Bindloss, Bhavika Mathur, Marisa Renzullo

Picture Research Susie Peachey, Ellen Root, Lucy Sienkowska, Oran Tarjan

Cartography Dominic Beddow, Simonetta Giori, James MacDonald, Reetu Pandey

DTP Jason Little, George Nimmo

Production Olivia Jeffries

Factchecker Lyn Parry

Proofreader Debra Wolter

Indexer Hilary Bird

Illustrator chrisorr.com

First edition created by DP Services, a division of Duncan Peterson Publishing Ltd.

Revisions Team
Avanika, Dipika Dasgupta, Mohammad Hassan, Sumita Khatwani, Shikha Kulkarni, Suresh Kumar, Bhavika Mathur, Halima Mohammed, Laura O'Brien, Kanika Praharaj, Vagisha Pushp, Rada Radojicic, Ruth Reisenberger, Rohit Rojal, Lucy Sara-Kelly, Taiyaba Khatoon, Anuroop Sanwalia, Ankita Sharma, Payal Sharotri, Mark Silas, Aakanksha Singh, Beverly Smart, Priyanka Thakur, Vinita Venugopal

Commissioned Photography Max Alexander, Alex Havret, Rough Guides/Greg Ward, Tony Souter

Picture Credits

The publisher would like to thank the following for their kind permission to reproduce their photographs:

Key: a-above; b-below/bottom; c-centre; f-far; l-left; r-right; t-top

Alamy Stock Photo: age fotostock/J.D. Dallet 55b; The Art Archive/Gianni Dagli Orti 96cla; Arterra Picture Library/Clement Philippe 21cl; David Bagnall 20bl, 21cra, 31tr; Sebastien Breham 4cl; BSIP SA/MAY 65tc; David Burton 71cl; Chronicle 50cr; John Elk III 80b; EPA/ Etienne Laurent 81tr; Keith Erskine 117crb; FALKENSTEINFOTO 51cla; Wayne Farrell 77crb; Patrick Forget 94cl, garfotos 65cla; Deborah Harmes 69br; Granger Historical Picture Archive / NYC 49tr; Hemis 52tl, / Arnaud Chicurel 30cl, 80t, /Betrand Rieger 99cra, 111tc, /Francis Cormon 87tl, 97bl, / Franck Guiziou 32cla, 34–5, 63tr, 66cla, 72t, 78tr, 98tl, 102tl, /Hervé Hughes 7tr, 39tl, 55cr, 110cla, /Stephane Lemaire 76b, /Rene Mattes 12cb, /Philippe Renault 33crb, /Jean-Daniel Sudres 70tr, 71br; imageBROKER/ gourmet-vision 72clb, /White Star/Guido Schiefer 74cb; incamerastock 23br; INTERFOTO/Fine Arts 17tl; Ivy Close Images 48b; Brian Jannsen 10cra; David Jones 22cr, 23cb, 33tl; John Kellerman 25cr; Les. Ladbury 63br; Lebrecht Music and Arts Photo Library 53tr; Lessay France/Steve Frost 103cra; Luise Berg-Ehlers 1; Photos 12/Gilles Targat 92tl; Rolf Richardson 36cr; robertharding/Jon Miller 58–9; Richard Semik 23tl; David South 104cra; Andrew Wilson 79tr, 115tl; World Pictures 114b; Tim Wright 81cl, Robert Zehetmayer 60br.

Bayeux-Bessin Tourisme: Claire Beauruel 18cl; Galerie Tapisserie de Bayeux avec autorisation spéciale de la Ville de Bayeux 10cl, 16–7; Photos Calvados/Gregory Wait 18br; JM Piel 36tl.

Galerie Tapisserie de Bayeux: 16clb.

Bridgeman Images: The Barnes Foundation, Philadelphia, Pennsylvania, USA *Mussel Fishers at* Berneval (1879) by Pierre Auguste Renoir 48tl; De Agostini Picture Library/ Bibliothèque Nationale De France, Paris *The Battle of Formigny, April 25, 1450*, miniature from *The Life of Charles VII by Jean Chartier* 46br; Jacques Prevert 51bl.

Calvados Tourisme: 64clb, 68cl, 70bl, 93cr, 95tl, 95bl.

Corbis: adoc-photos 47tr; AS400 DB 37b; Berliner Verlag/Archiv 47cl; Stefano Bianchetti 50tl; Massimo Borchi 88bc; Design Pics/Ian Cumming 60tl; Michael Freeman 19cl; The Gallery Collection 43b, /On the Beach at Trouville by Eugene Boudin 49cla; Hemis /Arnaud Chicurel 65b, /Francis Cormon 62cr, /Franck Guiziou 56t, 78b; Leemage 27cl, 46t; Frank Lukasseck 6l; Rivière/SoFood 73bl; Sygma 37r, /Sophie Bassouls 51tr; Topic Photo Agency 75bl.

Cité de la Mer: B.Almodovar 54bl.

Domaine St-Clair, Étretat: 91tr.

Dreamstime.com: Valentin Armianu 4clb; Briedys 13crb; Brighton 34clb; Musat Christian 67cla, 107crb; Claudio Giovanni Colombo 24cla, 26cr; Davidmartyn 103b; Delstudio 30–1; Demid 86cl; Ejespo 4crb; Eovsyannikova 12–3; Prochasson Frederic 20ca; Marius Godoi

32–3; Remus Grigore 98br; Jakezc 106b; Lukasz Janyst 2tl, 4t, 8–9, 31cr; Jorisvo 4b, 15bl, 16c, 17bl; Junkgirl 14crb; Kateryna Levchenko 108cla; Lubastock 86br; Francisco Javier Gil Oreja 11crb; Minnystock 1; Patrickwang 38–9; Peregrine 34cla, 108bl; Renaud Philippe 75tr; Philippehalle 2tr, 4cla, 20crb, 24br, 26clb, 35tl, 36bl, 38l, 44–5, 53l, 56bl, 88tr, 89cr, 97cr, 112b; Pierrot46 22cla; Ekaterina Pokrovsky 11crca; Pere Sanz 34br; Sergiyn 24–5, 85t; Jose I. Soto 14cla; Stevanzz 10br, 11tr; Topdeq 3tl, 4cr, 82–3; Tupungato 84tl; Ivonne Wierink 85cr; Xantana 67b, 100–1; Robert Zehetmayer 30br, 35br; Vladimir Zhuravlev 11tl; Zwawol 104bl.

Fondation Claude Monet, Giverny: 11br, 40cla, 40–1, 41tl, 43tl; Difalcone 41clb.

Getty Images: The Bridgeman Art Gallery/Musee des Beaux-Arts, Orleans, France *The Entrance of Joan of Arc into Orleans on 8th May 1429* by Jean-Jacques Scherrer 27b; Brigitte MERLE 76tr; John Elk 10clb, 23cra; Heritage Images 19bl; Jason's Travel Photography 28–9.

iStockphoto.com: guy-ozenne 7clb

Musée des impressionnismes Giverny: 42tl;Jean-Charles Louiset 42clb.

Normandie Tourisme: Thierry Houyel 105bl; C. Lehembre 107tl.

La Ferme des Mares: 109cr.

L'Epicier Olivier: 90cr.

Les Musilumieres de Sees: 116tr.

Rex by Shutterstock: Chriss Hellier 57cla; imageBROKER 73tr.

Robert Harding Picture Library: Richard Ashworth 93tr; Christian Goupi, 12bl, 13tl; Mel Longhurst 11clb, 39crb.

SuperStock: Hemis.fr 33c, /Bertrand Rieger 26tl.

Tourisme Orne: 3tr, 112cra, 113cla, 115crb, 118–9; F. Bouquerel 116tl; David Commenchal 62t; Manoir du Lys/Christian Vallee 74tl.

Cover

Front and spine: **Dreamstime.com:** Minnystock

Back: **Alamy Stock Photo:** tim gartside travel cla; funkyfood London – Paul Williams tl; **Dreamstime.com:** Janos Gaspar tr, Stevanzz crb; Minnystock b.

Pull Out Map Cover

Dreamstime.com: Minnystock

All other images © Dorling Kindersley

For further information see:
www.dkimages.com

First edition 2004

First published in Great Britain by
Dorling Kindersley Limited
DK, One Embassy Gardens, 8 Viaduct
Gardens, London SW11 7BW, UK

The authorised representative in the EEA is
Dorling Kindersley Verlag GmbH. Arnulfstr.
124, 80636 Munich, Germany

Published in the United States by
DK US, 1450 Broadway, Suite 801,
New York, NY 10018, USA

Copyright © 2004, 2022 Dorling
Kindersley Limited

A Penguin Random House Company

22 23 24 25 10 9 8 7 6 5 4 3 2 1

**Reprinted with revisions 2006, 2008, 2010,
2012, 2014, 2017, 2019, 2022**

A CIP catalogue record is available
from the British Library.

A catalogue record for this book is available
from the Library of Congress.

ISSN 1479-344X
ISBN 978-0-2414-6299-7

Printed and bound in China

www.dk.com

As a guide to abbreviations in visitor information blocks: **Adm** = *admission charge;* **D** = *dinner;* **L** = *lunch.*

MIX
Paper from
responsible sources
FSC™ C018179

Phrase Book

In an Emergency

Help!	Au secours!	oh sekoor
Stop!	Arrêtez!	aret-ay
Call…	Appelez…	apuh-lay
…a doctor!	…un médecin!	uñ medsañ
…an ambulance!	…une ambulance!	oon oñboo-loñs
…the police!	…la police!	lah poh-lees
…the fire brigade!	…les pompiers!	leh poñ-peeyay

Communication Essentials

Yes/No	Oui/Non	wee/noñ
Please	S'il vous plaît	seel voo play
Thank you	Merci	mer-see
Excuse me	Excusez-moi	exkoo-zay mwah
Hello	Bonjour	boñzhoor
Goodbye	Au revoir	oh ruh-vwar
Good night	Bonsoir	boñ-swar
What?	Quel, quelle?	kel, kel
When?	Quand?	koñ
Why?	Pourquoi?	poor-kwah
Where?	Où?	oo

Useful Phrases

How are you?	Comment allez-vous?	kom-moñ talay voo
Very well, Pleased to meet you.	Très bien, Enchanté de faire votre connaissance.	treh byañ, oñshoñ-tay duh fehr votr kon-ay-sans
Where is/are…?	Où est/sont…?	oo ay/soñ
Which way to..?	Quelle est la direction pour..?	kel ay lah deer-ek-syoñ poor
Do you speak English?	Parlez-vous anglais?	par-lay voo oñg-lay
I don't understand.	Je ne comprends pas.	zhuh nuh kom-proñ pah
I'm sorry.	Excusez-moi.	exkoo-zay mwah

Useful Words

big	grand	groñ
small	petit	puh-tee
hot	chaud	show
cold	froid	frwah
good	bon	boñ
bad	mauvais	moh-veh
open	ouvert	oo-ver
closed	fermé	fer-meh
left	gauche	gohsh
right	droit	drwah
entrance	l'entrée	l'on-tray
exit	la sortie	sor-tee
toilet	les toilettes	twah-let

Shopping

How much is it?	Ça fait combien?	sa fay kom-byañ
What time…	A quelle heure…	ah kel urr
…do you open?	…êtes-vous ouvert?	et-voo oo-ver
…do you close?	…êtes-vous fermé?	et-voo fer-may
Do you have?	Est-ce que vous avez?	es-kuh voo zavay

I would like …	Je voudrais…	zhuh voo-dray
Do you take credit cards?	Est-ce que vous acceptez les cartes de crédit?	es-kuh voo zaksept-ay leh kart duh krehdee
This one.	Celui-ci.	suhl-wee-see
That one.	Celui-là.	suhl-wee-lah
expensive	cher	shehr
cheap	pas cher, bon marché,	pah shehr, boñ mar-shay
size, clothes	la taille	tye
size, shoes	la pointure	pwañ-tur

Types of Shop

antique shop	le magasin d'antiquités	maga-zañ d'oñteekee-tay
bakery	la boulangerie	booloñ-zhuree
bank	la banque	boñk
bookshop	la librairie	lee-brehree
cake shop	la pâtisserie	patee-sree
cheese shop	la fromagerie	fromazh-ree
chemist	la pharmacie	farmah-see
department store	le grand magasin	groñ maga-zañ
delicatessen	la charcuterie	sharkoot-ree
gift shop	le magasin de cadeaux	maga-zañ duh kadoh
greengrocer	le marchand de légumes	mar-shoñ duh lay-goom
grocery	l'alimentation	alee-moñtasyoñ
market	le marché	marsh-ay
newsagent	le magasin de journaux	maga-zañ duh zhoor-no
post office	la poste, le bureau de poste, le PTT	pohst, booroh duh pohst, peh-teh-teh
supermarket	le supermarché	soo pehr-marshay
tobacconist	le tabac	tabah
travel agent	l'agence de voyages	l'azhoñs duh vwayazh

Sightseeing

art gallery	la galerie d'art	galer-ree dart
bus station	la gare routière	gahr roo-tee-yehr
cathedral	la cathédrale	katay-dral
church	l'église	l'aygleez
garden	le jardin	zhar-dañ
library	la bibliothèque	beebleeo-tek
museum	le musée	moo-zay
railway station	la gare (SNCF)	gahr (es-en-say-ef)
tourist office	l'office du tourisme	ohfees doo tooreesm
town hall	l'hôtel de ville	l'ohtel duh veel

Staying in a Hotel

Do you have a vacant room?	Est-ce que vous avez une chambre?	es-kuh voo-zavay oon shambr
I have a reservation.	J'ai fait une réservation.	zhay fay oon rayzehrva-syoñ
single room	la chambre à une personne	shambr ah oon pehr-son
twin room	la chambre à deux lits	shambr ah duh lee
room with a bath, shower	la chambre avec salle de bains, une douche	shambr avek sal duh bañ, oon doosh

double room, with a double bed	**la chambre à deux personnes, avec un grand lit**	shambr ah duh pehr-son avek un gronñ lee

Eating Out

Have you got a table?	**Avez-vous une table libre?**	avay-voo oon tahbl duh leebr
I want to reserve a table.	**Je voudrais réserver une table.**	zhuh voo-dray rayzehr-vay oon tahbl
The bill, please.	**L'addition, s'il vous plaît.**	l'adee-syoñ seel voo play
Waitress/ waiter	**Madame, Mademoiselle/ Monsieur**	mah-dam, mah-demwahzel/ muh-syuh
menu	**le menu, la carte**	men-oo, kart
fixed-price menu	**le menu à prix fixe**	men-oo ah pree feeks
cover charge	**le couvert**	koo-vehr
wine list	**la carte des vins**	kart-deh vañ
glass	**le verre**	vehr
bottle	**la bouteille**	boo-tay
knife	**le couteau**	koo-toh
fork	**la fourchette**	for-shet
spoon	**la cuillère**	kwee-yehr
breakfast	**le petit déjeuner**	puh-tee deh-zhuh-nay
lunch	**le déjeuner**	deh-zhuh-nay
dinner	**le dîner**	dee-nay
main course	**le plat principal**	plah prañsee-pal
starter, first course	**l'entrée, le hors d'oeuvre**	l'oñ-tray, or-duhvr
dish of the day	**le plat du jour**	plah doo zhoor
wine bar	**le bar à vin**	bar ah vañ
café	**le café**	ka-fay

Menu Decoder

baked	**cuit au four**	kweet oh foor
beef	**le boeuf**	buhf
beer	**la bière**	bee-yehr
boiled	**bouilli**	boo-yee
bread	**le pain**	pan
butter	**le beurre**	burr
cake	**le gâteau**	gah-toh
cheese	**le fromage**	from-azh
chicken	**le poulet**	poo-lay
chips	**les frites**	freet
chocolate	**le chocolat**	shoko-lah
coffee	**le café**	kah-fay
dessert	**le dessert**	deh-ser
duck	**le canard**	kanar
egg	**l'oeuf**	l'uf
fish	**le poisson**	pwah-ssoñ
fresh fruit	**le fruit frais**	frwee freh
garlic	**l'ail**	l'eye
grilled	**grillé**	gree-yay
ham	**le jambon**	zhoñ-boñ
ice, ice cream	**la glace**	glas
lamb	**l'agneau**	l'anyoh
lemon	**le citron**	see-troñ
fresh lemon juice	**le citron pressé**	see-troñ presseh
meat	**la viande**	vee-yand
milk	**le lait**	leh
mineral water	**l'eau minérale**	l'oh meeney-ral
oil	**l'huile**	l'weel

onions	**les oignons**	leh zonyoñ
orange juice	**l'orange pressée**	l'oroñzh presseh
pepper	**le poivre**	pwavr
pork	**le porc**	por
potatoes	**les pommes de terre**	pom duh tehr
rice	**le riz**	ree
roast	**rôti**	row-tee
salt	**le sel**	sel
sausage	**la saucisse**	sohsees
seafood	**les fruits de mer**	frwee duh mer
snails	**les escargots**	leh zes-kar-goh
soup	**la soupe, le potage**	soop, poh-tazh
steak	**le bifteck, le steak**	beef-tek, stek
sugar	**le sucre**	sookr
tea	**le thé**	tay
vegetables	**les légumes**	lay-goom
vinegar	**le vinaigre**	veenaygr
water	**l'eau**	l'oh
red wine	**le vin rouge**	vañ roozh
white wine	**le vin blanc**	vañ bloñ

Numbers

0	**zéro**	zeh-roh
1	**un, une**	uñ, oon
2	**deux**	duh
3	**trois**	trwah
4	**quatre**	katr
5	**cinq**	sañk
6	**six**	sees
7	**sept**	set
8	**huit**	weet
9	**neuf**	nerf
10	**dix**	dees
11	**onze**	oñz
12	**douze**	dooz
13	**treize**	trehz
14	**quatorze**	katorz
15	**quinze**	kañz
16	**seize**	sehz
17	**dix-sept**	dees-set
18	**dix-huit**	dees-weet
19	**dix-neuf**	dees-nerf
20	**vingt**	vañ
30	**trente**	tront
40	**quarante**	karoñt
50	**cinquante**	sañkoñt
60	**soixante**	swasoñt
70	**soixante-dix**	swasoñt-dees
80	**quatre-vingts**	katr-vañ
90	**quatre-vingt-dix**	katr-vañ-dees
100	**cent**	soñ
1,000	**mille**	meel

Time

one minute	**une minute**	oon mee-noot
one hour	**une heure**	oon urr
half an hour	**une demi-heure**	urr duh-me urr
one day	**un jour**	urr zhorr
Monday	**lundi**	luñ-dee
Tuesday	**mardi**	mar-dee
Wednesday	**mercredi**	mehrkruh-dee
Thursday	**jeudi**	zhuh-dee
Friday	**vendredi**	voñdruh-dee
Saturday	**samedi**	sam-dee
Sunday	**dimanche**	dee-moñsh

Normandy: Selected Town Index